IMAGES
of America

AFRICAN AMERICANS
OF CALVERT COUNTY

Joseph Evans has his picture taken at Sparrows Beach in the early 1960s. Sparrows Beach and Carrs' Beach, located in Annapolis, were two of the local destinations for African Americans in the 1950s and 1960s. Owned by sisters Florence Carr Sparrow and Elizabeth Carr Smith, the beaches often provided live entertainment with some of music's top artists of the day. (Joseph Evans.)

ON THE COVER: Clyde Jones eventually owned and operated a sawmill on his property in Sunderland. Jones and his father were sharecropping 20 acres in 1926 when he decided to move to Washington, D.C., in an attempt to better his economic circumstances. Working as a porter and truck driver, Jones and his wife, Pearl, saved enough money to put a down payment on 25 acres of land. Pictured are Martin Bailey (left) and John Jennings. Clyde Jones, Ernest Gaines, and Gaines Scott are also in the 1940s photograph but are not shown on the cover. (Ilean Ray.)

IMAGES
of America

AFRICAN AMERICANS
OF CALVERT COUNTY

William A. Poe

ARCADIA
PUBLISHING

Published by Arcadia Publishing
Charleston SC, Chicago IL, Portsmouth NH, San Francisco CA

Library of Congress Catalog Card Number: 2008924401

For all general information contact Arcadia Publishing at:
Telephone 843-853-2070
Fax 843-853-0044
E-mail sales@arcadiapublishing.com
For customer service and orders:
Toll-Free 1-888-313-2665

Visit us on the Internet at www.arcadiapublishing.com

This book is dedicated to my wife, Judi, and daughters, Audrey and Dakota, for their continuous support and inspiration; to my Mom for her encouragement and tremendous work ethic in raising three sons; to my Dad; and especially to my grandparents James and Gertrude Sale.

CONTENTS

ACKNOWLEDGMENTS

Every picture tells a story, and these photographs tell some of the stories of some of the people in our community. There are many more stories to capture and to share for future generations to enjoy and learn from.

I would like to thank all of those people in the community who entrusted me with their photographs as well as their stories.

An effort was made to notify the community in order for everyone to make a contribution to the project. Thank you to all of those who were able to do so.

Thank you to the people whose names appear at the end of the photograph captions and to those who are pictured in the photographs. Without your contribution, this book would not be possible.

Thank you to Patuxent Church and all of its members and to Rev. Tunde E. O. Davies for accepting me into your community.

Thanks to Lauren Bobier at Arcadia Publishing.

A special thanks to Kirsti Uunila (and Calvert County Planning and Zoning) for her continuing support and contributions.

Thank you to Dr. Marsha Plater for your enthusiasm, support, and contribution.

Thank you Karen Sykes, Denise Cherry, and the staff of the Linden House and Karen Maxey at the Board of Education.

Thanks to Jackie Niles-Cutlip, Debra Jones Riley, Michael Kent, Fran Poling, and the staff of *Calvert Life Magazine*.

Thanks to Ilean Ray for the cover image.

Thanks to all of my brothers and sisters in the community who have supported me.

Thank you to everyone in the Calvert County community who has supported this book as well as other projects of mine. Thanks to all of the storytellers who have inspired me, especially those in my family.

Information regarding the subjects and photographs was collected through various sources, including, but not limited to, personal interviews, newspaper articles, and historical documents.

Thanks to everyone who contributed in some form or fashion to this book. Particular gratitude goes to my brothers Rich, Mike, and Barry, and to Valerie, Linda, and Sonny.

Thanks to Yong Me and Frank Mowery.

Please forgive any errors that may have occurred in writing the captions.

The profits from the author's proceeds will go to the "I Am Somebody" Scholarship Fund, created in honor of Enoch Tyler and other farmers who were unable to complete their formal education in order to help support their families on the farm. The fund will help support continuing education for descendants of tenant farmers and sharecroppers. For further information on future projects that will support the scholarship fund or to make a donation, please contact William Poe at wjda@hotmail.com or write to William Poe at 9660 Howes Road, Dunkirk, MD 20754.

The "I Am Somebody" Scholarship Fund is part of I Am Somebody Productions and Films.

INTRODUCTION

I remember moving from the Washington, D.C., suburbs to Calvert County when I was 10 years old and praying for the day it would become a concrete walkway like the city I had just left. If I could turn back time and wish again, I would wish for the return of Calvert County's country way of life and those people who made it the unique and enriching place that romantics like me dream to be a part of.

It was not long after we had been living here that my thoughts began to change. As I ventured out into my community, walking to the little general store on the corner or trampling through the woods and stumbling upon an old abandoned wooden-framed house, I began to see the distinct characteristics of Calvert County. And as I took notice of the individual houses I passed along the way and the people who dwelled in the houses, I became intrigued. Soon after that, I found myself sitting on porches with those folks who piqued my interest; the more I sat talking with them, the more I came to admire their simple yet hardworking way of life.

Over the years, I spent a great deal of time with several gentlemen in my neighborhood who either had farmed in the past or who were still farming. I was in awe of their work ethic and listened closely to the stories they so willingly shared. I often walked home feeling as if I had been part of their past experiences.

As an adult, I continue to go out into the community to meet some of the longtime residents, most of whose families have been here for many generations. They are always forthcoming with personal anecdotes, often imparting simple words of wisdom to their guest.

I learned much from my hosts as I made my way through the roads of Calvert County, knocking on doors and asking for interviews. I am always greeted with colorblind eyes and made to feel welcome in their homes, more as a friend paying a social visit. I learned that although they endured many hardships during their lifetimes (some of which spanned almost an entire century), they never begrudged nor blamed any one person or particular group of people for any of their hardships. I learned some of their ancestors had been slaves in the very area that they now live, some recalling stories told directly to them by these ex-enslaved relatives.

I discovered that many families in the northern end of the county made their living as tobacco farmers, while families in the southern part of the county often made their living from the Chesapeake Bay and Patuxent River, harvesting the water's once plentiful oysters. And in the off-season of farming or being a waterman, the men would take construction jobs locally and out of the county as transportation improved. I learned that large numbers of the men served their country, some going off to war and some serving stateside. And many men and women decided not to farm as their parents had done. Some instead went to college and became professionals in many different occupational fields.

I was told the women often worked side by side with their husbands in the fields while raising their families. Some families consisted of a large number of offspring. Still others were teachers, some born and raised here, and others came from afar to educate. Some were midwives who would be summoned to a home in the middle of the night or to the local hospital to help deliver a child.

Some worked at restaurants and the local beaches, while others worked as nannies, helping to raise the children of white families, families who thought highly of their black assistants.

I learned that a number of these hardworking men and women went to great lengths to see that their children became formally educated so they would not have to struggle as they had done. Many in this community are God-fearing, God-loving people whose faith has often been put to the test, yet they still continue to believe.

I realized over time that to be accepted as part of this community is a blessing and means you must be doing something right. And lastly, I learned that some of life's simple lessons often come from some of the wisest, yet unassuming people, the seasoned citizens, and are there for all of us to learn—lessons I take with me on my journey: If you treat people the way you want to be treated, then there is a good chance they will treat you the same. If you take the time to show an interest in the lives of others, they will respond favorably and with appreciation. Most of the treasured moments you may ever experience can be found in simple settings with some of life's most interesting people. And some of life's most simple pleasures are right here, perhaps on your neighbor's front porch.

As I look at what some of these folks did without and many still do without, I know contentment can be found in simplicity.

I learned much on this journey, not only about the people represented in this book, but also about myself.

This is a community of family, whether by blood, marriage, or friendship. It is unique and still thrives and is a special place to live.

This book is a tribute to these wonderful folks of this county who have invested, sacrificed, and improved our quality of life by their mere existence among us.

One

SERVICEMEN

Harrison Jones enlisted in the U.S. Army in October 1917. After training intensely at Camp Meade in Maryland, in June 1918, Private 1st Class Jones and the 351st Field Artillery, Supply Company, left for Brest, France. Once there, the regiment trained at the Artillery School of Fire La Courtine. In October, the 351st left for the front as part of the 167th Field Artillery Brigade. They engaged in the frontal attack on Corny on November 10. (Jones family.)

Rachel Chase wed Thomas Gray in 1869, four years after he was discharged from the U.S. Colored Troops. Although she had remarried after his death in 1873, Chase still qualified to receive her late husband's veteran's benefits. In 1889, Chase began petitioning to collect her widow's pension. These documents are only two of many that were filed during the next 41 years seeking arrears of pay as an heir to Gray. Other documents filed were notarized letters from local residents stating that Chase was indeed married to Gray. In 1930, Chase was finally awarded $40 a month. (Jones family.)

Pvt. Thomas Gray served from March 1864 to December 1865 in the U.S. Colored Troops. He served in Company C of the 39th Regiment, organized in Baltimore in March 1864. His name, along with 209,145 others, can be located on the Wall of Honor at the African American Civil War Monument in Washington, D.C. Gray died in 1873 from an injury received in battle at Petersburg. He is believed to be buried somewhere on the family farm. (Jones family.)

CERTIFICATE OF HONOR

Thomas Gray

39th Regiment, U.S. Colored Infantry

Organized at Baltimore, Md., March 22-31, 1864. This name may be located on Wall C, Plaque 54 on the Wall of Honor at the African American Civil War Monument. This monument is located at the intersection of 10th and U Street N.W., Washington, D.C.

A grateful nation finally pays tribute to the 209,145 troops who helped save the nation, end slavery and start America on a struggle for freedom that continues today.

Dr. Frank Smith, Founding Director
Civil War Memorial Freedom Foundation

For more information about this soldier, please visit our website at www.afroamcivilwar.org. You may also wish to search the database for your family name.

This manumission document from 1864 releases James Egins from all services to his owner, John Sedwick, guaranteeing his freedom. The government compensated slave owners for their "property" when slaves enlisted to fight in the Civil War. Although Egins had enlisted in October 1863, his owner did not file the manumission document until June 1864. Egins enlisted in the 9th Regiment of the U.S. Colored Troops. Other documents list $300 as compensation. (Calvert County Planning and Zoning.)

Albert Gantt was born in Calvert County in 1843, the son of James and Charlotte Gantt. According to his family, Albert was enslaved by Dr. John C. Parker. In 1864, Gantt enlisted in the U.S. Colored Troops. He served in several engagements in the war, including Petersburg. Discharged in Texas in 1866, he returned to Maryland and worked in Baltimore. He saved enough money to return to Calvert and buy a farm, where he lived with his wife, Aleatha. He was a frequent master of ceremonies for community celebrations and is buried at the Brooks United Methodist Cemetery. (Both, Johnson family.)

Several months after World War I ended, a celebration for African American servicemen of Calvert County was given honoring their heroic efforts overseas. Local churches would sometimes host events, and local officials (white) often addressed the attendees. In both 1919 newspaper clippings shown here, African American Civil War veteran Albert Gantt presided on selected committees. It is estimated that 367,710 African American men were called under the Selective Service Draft Regulations between the years 1917 and 1918. The quality of training and facilities for African Americans were substandard compared to that given to white servicemen preparing for war. (Both, *Calvert Gazette*.)

SOLDIERS' CELEBRATION
AND
HOME COMING.

The people of Calvert County (colored) will give in honor of the Calvert Soldiers, Marines and Sailors who participated in the late world war an

ENTERTAINMENT AND CELEBRATION
AT
MT. OLIVE M. E. CHURCH,

Near Prince Frederick, Calvert County, Md.,

Saturday, September 20th, 1919,
AT 12 M.

A BAND OF MUSIC

will be on the grounds and furnish music throughout the entertainment.

Mr William A. Randall will deliver an address of welcome and Hon. John P. Briscoe and Hon. Thomas Parran and others will deliver addresses for the occasion.

The people of the county generally are requested to aid in making the occasion one of the greatest in the history of the county.

The Soldiers are requested to appear in uniform.

Executive Committee for Calvert County:

Albert Gantt, John W. Brown, James Sewell, Clem Heigh, Mrs. Olivia Smith, Mrs. David Brooks, Mrs. Elizabeth Scott.

Colored Soldiers Honored.

A Soldiers' Luncheon prepared by the leading colored people of Island Creek neighborhood was held at the hall near Brooks' Church on Wednesday afternoon. The colored soldiers who have returned from overseas and camps were guests, and a bountiful repast was served them. The soldiers gave an exhibition drill and told some interesting accounts of their experiences. Albert Gantt, an old Civil War veteran, was master of ceremonies. Addresses were made by States Attorney J. Frank Parran and Arthur W. Dowell.

Joseph Wesley Jones, shown in 1945, entered the U.S. Army Air Force when he was 19 years old. He spent his tour of duty at Williams Field in Chandler, Arizona. A special vehicle operator while he served, Jones went on to open a school bus contracting service in 1955. His son Cameron took over the business in 2003. Jones currently resides at the Charlotte Hall Veterans' Home. (Jones family.)

ENLISTED RECORD AND REPORT OF SEPARATION

HONORABLE DISCHARGE

Joseph Wesley Jones was honorably discharged in 1946 after two years and four months of service. Jones received a hardship discharge after the war was over to assist in operating the family's tobacco farm. When the off-season of growing tobacco arrived, Jones would "go up the road" to Washington, D.C., to work as a carpenter. This was typical for the farming community of Calvert County. (Jones family.)

Born to Earnest and Florence Plater in 1921, Roland Plater left for military service in December 1942. Serving in the army as a lineman, Plater was injured in 1943 after he fell from a telephone pole in the Philippines. He recovered at Luzon Philippines Hospital on Wheels but never received any disability pay for his injuries. Plater was honorably discharged in February 1946 as a technician fourth grade. (Marsha Plater.)

The second child of Maurice and Agnes Brooks, Arthur was born in 1913. While stationed in Solomons, Maryland, serving in the armed forces, Brooks was constantly visited by his sisters. Maurice Brooks warned his daughters, "Don't keep going down there because they will know he's local and ship him out." Not long after, Brooks was shipped out. He died of tuberculosis and is buried in Arlington Cemetery. He is pictured here with friend Emma Jackson in the 1940s. (Marsha Plater.)

Until the time he was drafted, Norman Gray Jr., son of Norman and Rosa Gray, worked in the construction trade alongside his father. At age 19, Gray (pictured here in 1943) left Calvert County to serve his country in World War II. (Gray family.)

A private first class in the army with the 370th Infantry, 92nd Division, Company F, Norman Gray Jr. was killed in action on September 15, 1944, in Italy. The American Legion Gray-Ray Post in Port Republic is named in honor of Gray and Roosevelt Ray. They were the first two African American soldiers from Calvert County to be killed in World War II. Gray was buried in Italy, and Ray's body was returned home for burial. (Gray family.)

Drafted in 1942 at the age of 23, Leroy Berry had just graduated from Eckels College of Embalming in Philadelphia. After completing his basic training in Fort Meade, Berry served with the Medical Detachment 366th Infantry Regiment. He had requested to be part of a medical unit, and because

of his recent studies to become a mortician, his request was granted. Berry is pictured standing fourth from left in the second row. (Leroy Berry.)

ENLISTED RECORD AND REPORT OF SEPARATION
HONORABLE DISCHARGE

1. LAST NAME - FIRST NAME - MIDDLE INITIAL		2. ARMY SERIAL NO.	3. GRADE	4. ARM OR SERVICE	5. COMPONENT
BERRY - LEROY E		33 180 554	TEC 4	MD	AUS
6. ORGANIZATION		7. DATE OF SEPARATION	8. PLACE OF SEPARATION SEPARATION CENTER		
MED DET 366TH INF		11 NOV 45	FORT GEORGE G MEADE MD		

9. PERMANENT ADDRESS FOR MAILING PURPOSES	10. DATE OF BIRTH	11. PLACE OF BIRTH
DARES POST OFFICE CALVERT CO MD	20 JUL 18	DARES MD

12. ADDRESS FROM WHICH EMPLOYMENT WILL BE SOUGHT	13. COLOR EYES	14. COLOR HAIR	15. HEIGHT	16. WEIGHT	17. NO. DEPEND.
SEE 9	BROWN	BLACK	5'4"	130 LBS.	1

18. RACE			19. MARITAL STATUS			20. U.S. CITIZEN		21. CIVILIAN OCCUPATION AND NO.
WHITE	NEGRO X	OTHER (specify)	SINGLE	MARRIED X	OTHER (specify)	YES X	NO	EMBALMER 0-65.10

MILITARY HISTORY

22. DATE OF INDUCTION	23. DATE OF ENLISTMENT	24. DATE OF ENTRY INTO ACTIVE SERVICE	25. PLACE OF ENTRY INTO SERVICE
9 APR 42		9 APR 42	FORT MEADE MD

SELECTIVE SERVICE DATA	26. REGISTERED YES X / NO	27. LOCAL S.S. BOARD NO. 29	28. COUNTY AND STATE PHILADELPHIA PA	29. HOME ADDRESS AT TIME OF ENTRY INTO SERVICE ANNAPOLIS MD

30. MILITARY OCCUPATIONAL SPECIALTY AND NO.	31. MILITARY QUALIFICATION AND DATE (i.e. infantry, aviation and marksmanship badges, etc.)
MEDICAL TECHNICIAN 409.	MEDICAL BADGE

32. BATTLES AND CAMPAIGNS
GO33WD45:   ROME ARNO   NORTH APENNINES   PO VALLEY

33. DECORATIONS AND CITATIONS
AMERICAN THEATER SERVICE RIBBON   EUROPEAN AFRICAN MIDDLE EASTERN SERVICE RIBBON   GOOD CONDUCT MEDAL   WORLD WAR II VICTORY RIBBON

34. WOUNDS RECEIVED IN ACTION
NONE

35. LATEST IMMUNIZATION DATES				36. SERVICE OUTSIDE CONTINENTAL U.S. AND RETURN		
SMALLPOX	TYPHOID	TETANUS	OTHER (specify)	DATE OF DEPARTURE	DESTINATION	DATE OF ARRIVAL
FEB45	SEP45	JAN44	TYPHUS MAR45	28 MAR 44	MOROCCO	6 APR 44

37. TOTAL LENGTH OF SERVICE				38. HIGHEST GRADE HELD			
CONTINENTAL SERVICE			FOREIGN SERVICE			20 OCT 45	UNITED STATES 6 NOV 45
YEARS	MONTHS	DAYS	YEARS	MONTHS	DAYS		
1	11	24	1	7	9	TEC 4	23877-DC

39. PRIOR SERVICE
NONE

40. REASON AND AUTHORITY FOR SEPARATION
CONVENIENCE OF THE GOVERNMENT RR 1-1 (DEMOBILIZATION) AR 615-365 15 DEC 44

41. SERVICE SCHOOLS ATTENDED	42. EDUCATION (Years)		
NONE	Grammar	High School 4	College

PAY DATA

43. LONGEVITY FOR PAY PURPOSES			44. MUSTERING OUT PAY		45. SOLDIER DEPOSITS	46. TRAVEL PAY	47. TOTAL AMOUNT, NAME OF DISBURSING OFFICER
YEARS 3	MONTHS	DAYS	TOTAL $100.00	THIS PAYMENT $100.00	NONE	$5.75	$359.37 C A PEARSON CAPTAIN FD

INSURANCE NOTICE

IMPORTANT: IF PREMIUM IS NOT PAID WHEN DUE OR WITHIN THIRTY-ONE DAYS THEREAFTER, INSURANCE WILL LAPSE.   MAKE CHECKS OR MONEY ORDERS PAYABLE TO THE TREASURER OF THE U. S. AND FORWARD TO COLLECTIONS SUBDIVISION, VETERANS ADMINISTRATION, WASHINGTON 25, D. C.

48. KIND OF INSURANCE			49. HOW PAID			50. Effective Date of Allotment Discontinuance	51. Date of Next Premium Due (One month after 50)	52. PREMIUM DUE EACH MONTH	53. INTENTION OF VETERAN TO		
Nat. serv. X	U.S. Govt.	None	Allotment	Direct to V. A. X		31 OCT 45	30 NOV 45	$6.70	Continue	Continue Only X	Discontinue

54.

55. REMARKS (This space for completion of above items or entry of other items specified in W. D. Directives)
LAPEL BUTTON ISSUED   NO TIME LOST UNDER AW 107

ASR SCORE 66

RIGHT THUMB PRINT

56. SIGNATURE OF PERSON BEING SEPARATED	57. PERSONNEL OFFICER (Type name, grade and organization - signature)
Leroy E. Berry	MILDRED H LOVEITT 1ST LT WAC *Mildred H. Loveitt*

Leroy Berry departed the United States for Casablanca, Morocco, in March 1944. This enlistment record shows Berry served in three battles and campaigns: Rome Arno, North Apennines, and Po Valley. He was awarded three ribbons and one medal during his enlistment. On two separate occasions, shells landed within yards of Berry but were duds. "Twice I should have been dead," he said. Berry retired as a mortician in 1989. (Leroy Berry.)

Kinsey Jones was born in the Chesapeake Beach area and was drafted during World War II, becoming a navy Seabee. The Seabees were formed in 1942 under the authority of Adm. Ben Moreell, becoming part of the Naval Construction Unit and often tasked with building bridges and roads. Moreell coined the Seabees motto: "Construimus, Batuimus," meaning, "We Build, We Fight." In this 1940s photograph, Jones is somewhere in the South Pacific. (Timothy Jones.)

Born in Owings in 1932, Leroy Lorenzo Holland enlisted in the U.S. Army in 1950 just after graduating from Sampson Brooks High School, the same year he is pictured. A member of the Airborne Division, he was stationed in Germany for a tour of duty. After completing his army enlistment, he volunteered to join the U.S. Air Force. Following his honorable discharge, Holland went to work in a Washington, D.C., hospital as a cook. (Eloise Ray.)

Mickey (née Locks) Ray was drafted in the U.S. Army (and is pictured here) in 1953. Ray was stationed at Fort Pickett, Virginia, for basic training before being sent to Korea. Ray just missed the Korean War conflict. He spent 16 months overseas as a medic. After returning home, Ray took a job in Baltimore with Giant Food and retired after 39 years of service. (Mickey Ray.)

Born in 1934 to Guy and Hattie Brooks, Herbert Lee attended W. S. Brooks High School. His math teacher, Warrick Hill, recalls Brooks and several of Brooks's family members eating lunch together in his homeroom class. After being discharged from the army, Brooks went to New York, where he was employed as a union iron worker. Brooks, shown here in the early 1950s, died at age 37. He and his wife, Genevive, had no children. (Marsha Plater.)

Until 1960, Kinsey Jones II worked on the family farm in Dunkirk, helping to raise tobacco. At that time, Jones was called to military service, where he spent the next 22 years working his way up the military ladder, achieving the rank of sergeant major in the army. Jones spent one and a half years of his service in Vietnam and is pictured here in the early 1980s. (Timothy Jones.)

Before being drafted into the army in 1955, Jesse Reid completed his college degree at the University of Maryland Eastern Shore. Majoring in agricultural education with a minor in science, Reid taught school at his alma mater, Brooks High School, after completing his enlistment in 1957. In 1960, he began a school bus contracting business, which is still in operation today. (Reid family.)

Jesse Jones Reid was inducted into the Maryland National Guard on March 17, 1980. After completing his basic training in Fort Dix, New Jersey, Reid went on to Fort Leonardwood, Missouri, and Fort Belvoir, Virginia. Monthly drills were held at the county's local armory in Prince Frederick. He served as a combat engineer and truck driver until he was honorably discharged in 1986. (Reid family.)

In 1959, after completing his education at Oakwood College, Wilson Leon Holland joined the army. His active duty obligation lasted through 1962. While stationed in West Germany, Holland became the father of twin daughters. Achieving the rank of specialist 4, Holland was honorably discharged in 1966 after fulfilling four years in the army reserve. In 1967, a year after he had been discharged and returned to Calvert County, Holland married Virginia Offer, becoming the stepfather to six children. His wife passed away in 1988, and Holland died in 2004. (Marsha Plater.)

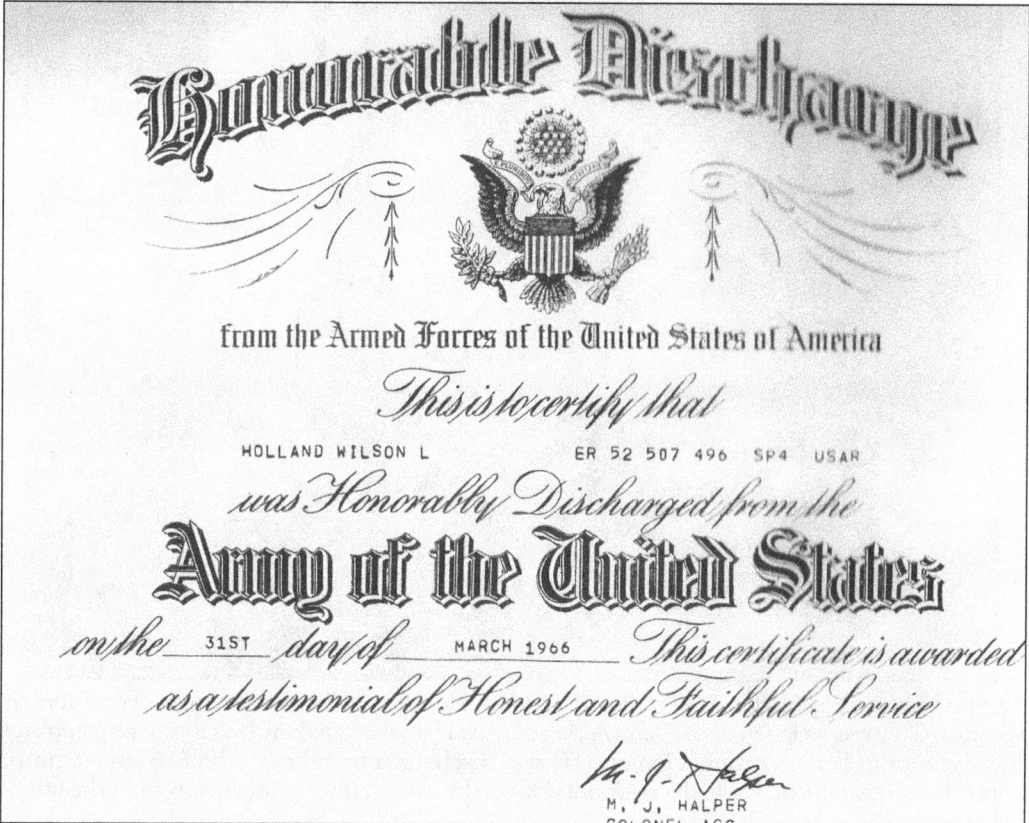

Honorable Discharge

from the Armed Forces of the United States of America

This is to certify that

HOLLAND WILSON L   ER 52 507 496   SP4   USAR

was Honorably Discharged from the

Army of the United States

on the 31ST day of MARCH 1966 This certificate is awarded as a testimonial of Honest and Faithful Service

M. J. HALPER
COLONEL AGC

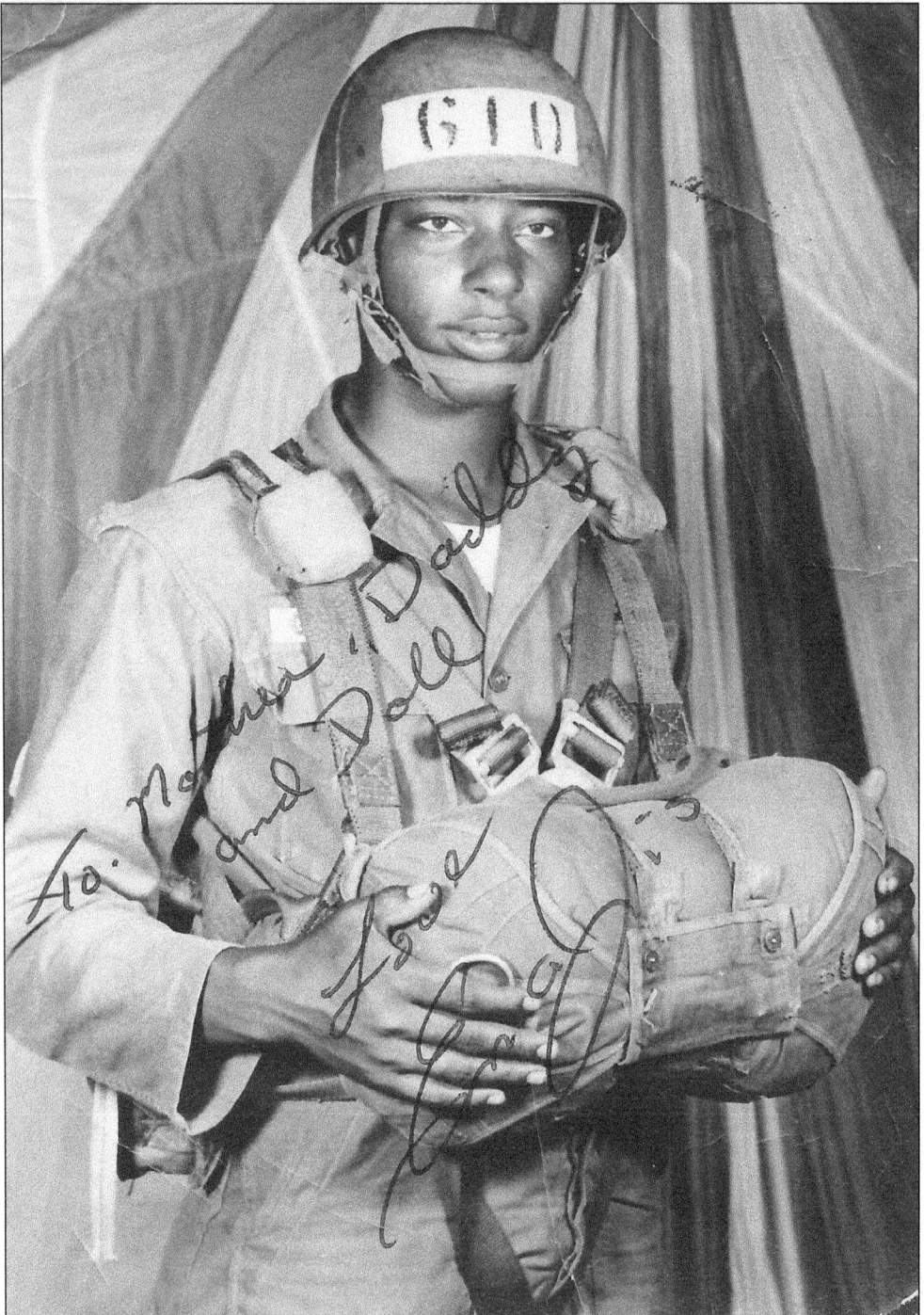

Englis Gray enlisted in the army in February 1963. He spent his basic training in Fort Gordon, Georgia. Gray was assigned to the 82nd Airborne, 82nd Battalion, in Fort Bragg after he completed jump school in Fort Benning, Georgia. He was discharged in February 1966 as an air traffic controller. Gray returned to Calvert County, where he eventually became involved in the family construction business. (Gray family.)

Upon graduating high school in 1964, Donald Carroll enlisted in the U.S. Army. After leaving Fort Meade, Maryland, Carroll was assigned to Germany as his next duty station, where he was a wheel vehicle mechanic. Next he was sent to Vietnam, where he drove an ambulance for the medical unit. With his enlistment complete, Carroll eventually went to work for UPS, where he retired. (Madora Carroll.)

Inducted into the army in 1964, Clifton William Russell proceeded to Fort Gordon, Georgia, for basic training. After completing engineering school in St. Louis, Missouri, he was sent overseas to Germany and then served one tour of duty in Vietnam. After being discharged in 1967, Russell was employed for several years at the Naval Ordinance Base in Indianhead before retiring from UPS in 1991. (Viola Kent.)

27

Ralph Parran was employed at a men's clothier in Washington, D.C., when he was drafted in 1966. After his induction in Baltimore, Parran left for Parris Island, South Carolina, to complete his basic training. Upon graduation from boot camp, he was assigned to 2nd Battalion, 6th Marines, at Camp Lejeune, North Carolina. He was an 0311, otherwise known as an infantryman. (Parran family.)

During his enlistment from 1966 to 1968, Ralph Parran was assigned to the Fleet Marine Force, where he went out to sea for six-month intervals. While aboard the USS *Guadalcanal* touring the Caribbean Sea, Parran was one of the ship's barbers. He also served on the USS *Montreal* in the Mediterranean Sea. His favorite ports-of-call were Naples, Italy, and Barcelona, Spain. (Parran family.)

Just after graduation from Calvert High School in 1967, Warren "Sammy" Evans (pictured here the following year) was drafted into the army. After completing his basic training in Fort Bragg, North Carolina, Evans went on to Army Infantry Training in Fort Ord, California. He served a 14-month tour of duty in Korea before being honorably discharged in 1969. (Sheenae Evans.)

James Richard Jones enlisted in the navy in 1971 (when he is pictured). His basic training was completed in Great Lakes, Illinois, and after he completed "A" School, he became an electronic repair technician working on radar and guided missile systems. Honorably discharged in 1977 as an E-5, Jones is still active in military retirement. (Timothy Jones.)

In 1973, when this image was taken, Timothy Jones was part of the selective service program. He decided to enlist instead, "Because if you got drafted, you typically had to go in the Army. So I decided to volunteer so I could pick which branch of the service I could go in." Jones went into the navy, where he was an engineman. He received orders to go to Vietnam, but America's involvement was coming to a close so he remained stateside. (Timothy Jones.)

Continuing in the tradition of his father, Timothy, and grandfather Kinsey, Patrick Jones enlisted in the U.S. Navy shortly after graduating from Northern High School. Jones received his boot camp training as well as "A" School instruction in Great Lakes, Illinois. He currently resides in Florida and is employed as an electrician. (Timothy Jones.)

Above, Michael Gayhart Kent stands outside the family home in Huntingtown in 1984. Kent interrupted his college education to become a signalman in the navy. He continued his education while in the military reserves, graduating from the University of Maryland at Baltimore Law School in 1984. Kent was then commissioned an ensign in the Judge Advocate Corps. He began his law career in 1985 with the Baltimore State's Attorney Office. (Viola Kent.)

"I just wanted to push it. Be all that I could be. I wanted to push it to the limit," remarked Robert M. Carter III when asked why he joined the 82nd Airborne Division and became a Ranger. Carter was a demolition specialist in Desert Storm, helping to sweep the mine fields. He was deployed to Honduras and Bolivia, where his unit worked closely with the Drug Enforcement Agency. (Carter family.)

James Henry Carroll Jr. enlisted in the U.S. Marine Corps in 1962. Carroll, originally from Calvert, left for New York when he was 16 years old. After completing boot camp at Parris Island, South Carolina, Carroll was stationed in Puerto Rico. Upon being discharged, he returned to New York, where he drove a truck for the Christian Dior Company. He died in 1977 and is buried at Young's Methodist Church. (Madora Carroll.)

The son of Allan and Cleo Brown, Allan Anthony Brown enlisted in the army in 1980 after graduating from Northern High School. He completed Advanced Individual Training (AIT) School in Alabama, where he became a military policeman. Stationed in Berlin, Germany, for 18 months, Brown not only patrolled the base, but also had jurisdiction in the city of Berlin, working with the German police. He was discharged in 1984. (Brown family.)

Two

MATRIMONY

Charles Kinslow and Jill Amspacher were wed on May 6, 1978, in Lusby. Kinslow was one of the first of four students to integrate Calvert High School in 1963. He, along with Blanche Jones, Patricia Morsell, and James Hutchins, was required to take a battery of standardized tests for class placement and was informed by the superintendent that he would make Cs and Ds on the tests. He had volunteered to attend Calvert in order to support James Hutchins. He experienced the harshest of racial prejudices. "Calvert was my personal Vietnam," he said. He graduated in the top 10 of the class of 1966. Upon graduation, he attended Maryland State College, an all-black school, "to escape foolishness of racial bigotry only to discover that foolishness has no color barrier." On his marriage, he states, "One of the best decisions [I] ever made because it led to a right relationship with Christ." The Kinslows have two daughters, Bailey and Jessica. "The lives of our daughters continue to reflect that racial bigotry and injustice exists and is not colorblind," he says. (Kinslow family.)

Columbus Ray descends the staircase in his home in Huntingtown with daughter Alma Teresa on her wedding day. A daughter of tobacco farming parents, Alma married Howard F. Malloy Jr. in June 1964. They had two children, Kimberly Cherisse and Timothy Drew. Pictured from left to right are Donna Watts, Georgine Byers, Patricia Gorman, Genevive Johnson, and Mary Ray. (Eloise Ray.)

While driving from their New York home to Calvert County to visit her parents, Alma and her entire family perished in the Christian Creek in Delaware when their car lost control on an icy road in 1970. They are buried at Bethel Way of the Cross in Huntingtown. (Eloise Ray.)

Mr. and Mrs. E. Columbus Ray

request the honour of your presence

at the marriage of their daughter

Alma Teresa

to

Mr. Howard F. Malloy, Jr.

on Saturday, the twenty-seventh of June

Nineteen hundred and sixty-four

at three o'clock in the afternoon

478 Breezes Point Road

Hunting Town, Maryland

Reception
immediately following the ceremony

Russell Reid Jr. and Phyllis Greene met when Phyllis's father, Leroy Greene, moved his family from their tenant farming home to his newly purchased farm on Ponds Wood Road in 1949. The two played together as elementary school children and began dating in their teens. They were married in 1960 and have four children. This photograph was taken in 1958 at Reid's grandfather's house. (Phyllis Reid.)

Joseph Evans and Hattie Spriggs were married in Lothian in 1952. They met while attending the same elementary school in Dunkirk. Hattie was employed as a domestic worker most of her life. When they first married, Joe worked the land next to where his father farmed. In the early 1960s, Joe began his career as a bricklayer. They have two sons, Reginald and Joseph. (Joseph Evans.)

Bertha Harrod and Cephas Wallace were married in 1952. Harrod was a domestic worker in the southern part of Calvert County for various families over the years. Wallace was drafted into the U.S. Army in August 1945. He was a rifleman in the infantry and received the Victory Medal and Good Conduct Medal during his enlistment. This photograph at Sparrows Beach was taken sometime during the 1950s. (Gladys Jones.)

After his military service, Cephas Wallace became a carpenter. With a small wood shop behind his home in Port Republic, Wallace began making furniture. In the late 1960s, he started to make headstones for relatives whose grave sites had never been properly marked. Local people also requested his services. His headstones can be seen throughout the county at local cemeteries and churches. Wallace passed away in 2000. (Gladys Jones.)

In November 1962, Therman Gray Sr. and Carthella "Carolyn" Parran exchanged wedding vows at Patuxent United Methodist Church. Their reception was held at the home of the bride's parents, Alice and Hamilton Parran Sr., in Dares Beach. Food for approximately 250 guests was prepared in the basement by "Big Momma" Alice Parran. The Grays have three children: Pam, Angela, and Therman Jr. (Gray family.)

The Gray family is pictured in front of Wards Memorial Methodist Church in the late 1970s. From left to right are (first row) daughter Shirley, matriarch Helen Gray, and daughter Ilean; (second row) sons Charles, Alvin, and Therman. The occasion on this day was the marriage of Alvin's son, Vaughn. Helen, Shirley, and Alvin have since passed away. (Gray family.)

Guffrie Smith Jr. and Catherine "Casey" Cheers exchanged vows on July 11, 1964, in Church Hill, Maryland. A month earlier, Smith had graduated from Bowie State College. The couple met in 1961 when Cheers arrived as a freshman. Smith recalls, "We were married by Casey's pastor in a small ceremony with a few family members in attendance. It had to be the hottest day of the year. I couldn't stop perspiring." (Guffrie Smith.)

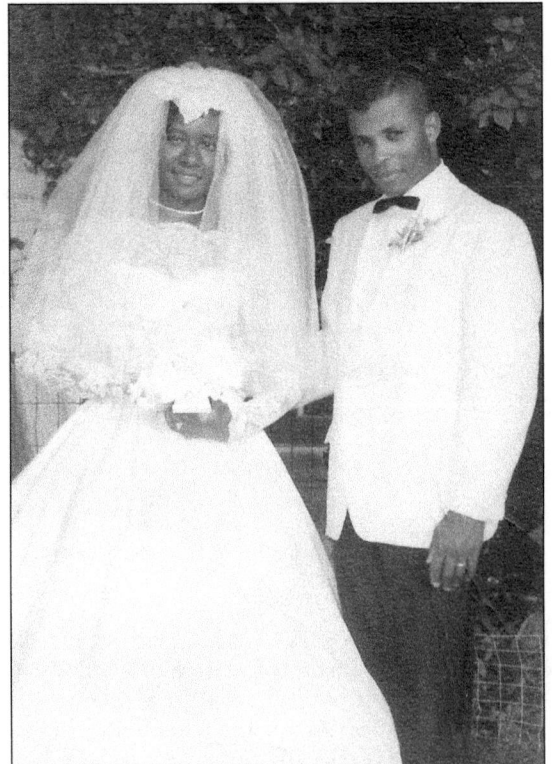

Kinsey Jones II met his wife while he was stationed in Fort Dix, New Jersey. He and Eleanor Figaro of Louisiana were married in 1966 in Massachusetts. After retiring from military service in 1982, Jones became a ROTC teacher in the Washington, D.C., public school system. (Timothy Jones.)

Eleanora Hurley and Ralph Parran were joined in holy matrimony on September 21, 1968. Flanking the bride and groom on the left are the bride's parents, Alvin Hurley Sr. and Helen, and grandmother Ada Morsell. The groom's parents, Alice and Hamilton Parran Sr., are to the right. The best man was Alfus Parran, and the maid of honor was Bertina Hurley. The ceremony was held at Ward's United Methodist Church. (Parran family.)

This family photograph of the Parrans was taken in the early 1980s. Pictured from left to right are (first row) Samantha, Ralph Jr., and Eleanora; (second row) Ramona, Ralph Sr., and Tanya. All four of the Parran children graduated from Calvert High School and live locally. (Parran family.)

After his discharge form the U.S. Army, Warren Evans returned to Calvert County, where he met Ruth Jones. Jones had just graduated from Calvert High School when she began dating Evans. They were married at the home of a Reverend Collins in Mutual in 1972. They have two children, Warren Jr. and Sheenae. The Evanses have been married 36 years and reside in Huntingtown. (Sheenae Evans.)

On the back of a Polaroid picture, Warren Evans wrote these words to his wife-to-be, Ruth: "To My Future Wife, May your heart and mine be filled with the happiness that life brings—so let's continue being the way we are so we would have a successful future to come." (Sheenae Evans.)

Dorothy Smothers and David Gray were married in 1938. They purchased a 150-acre farm in 1939. David, following in the footsteps of his father, Norman, owned a local construction company. He built the Gray's Alemeda Club (a local food and music establishment) in the 1940s and ran it until the mid-1950s. Smothers was born in Baltimore and came to Mill Creek on a steamboat at the age of two to live with her grandfather and mother. They had five children. (Dorothy Gray.)

Married in 1941, Alice Jones and Hamilton Parran Sr. raised three sons and a daughter. This photograph, taken at Sparrows Beach in the late 1950s, is one of many summer visits the Parrans made to the Chesapeake Bay. "Big Momma," as Alice was affectionately known, was a worthy matron of Carroll Chapter No. 22, Order of the Eastern Star. Hamilton was a loyal employee of Joseph and Jean Rose of Rose Haven for more than 40 years. (Dorothy Gray.)

These photographs of Allan and Cleo Brown were taken in 1975 at Patuxent United Methodist Church. On Valentine's Day in 2000, Brown was asked by church members to tell how he and his wife met. A portion of his letter reads, "It was the start of a new year at Brooks High School, and I spotted this girl getting off the bus with the long black pony tail. I recall taking one of my friends to see what I thought was a very cute girl catch the bus several times, but I never approached her. When I received the letter at school at the end of the day, I was so very excited. I could not believe this girl I had been admiring but had never approached, was now interested in me. . . . I recall walking down in the woods where there were no distractions to read this letter." The Browns celebrated their 50th anniversary in 2008. (Brown family.)

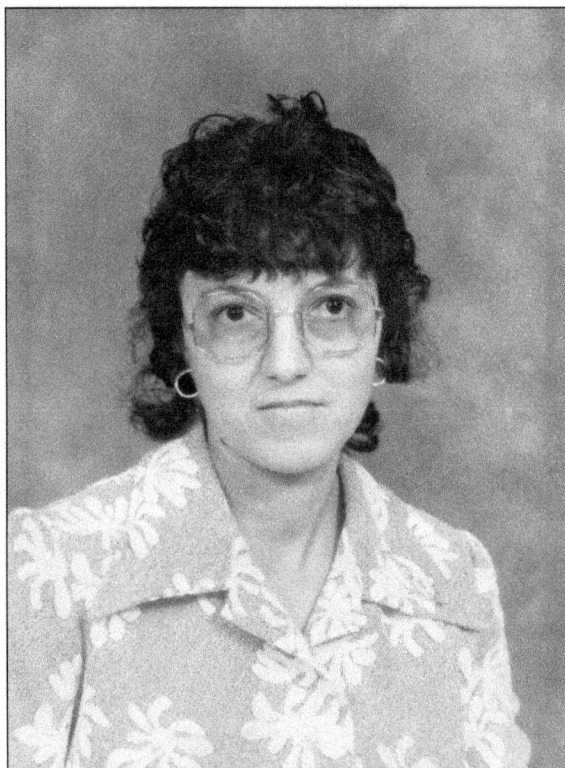

Three

EDUCATION

Dr. William Sampson Brooks was born to Robert and Margie Brooks in 1865. He was raised on a farm in Lower Marlboro and attended public school in Calvert County. Graduating from Centenary Biblical Institute (Morgan Institute) in 1892, Dr. Brooks began his career as a pastor and lecturer. His broad interests lead to his overseas travel to such places as Sweden, Norway, and the British Isles. He also spent time in Jerusalem and Liberia. He authored several books, including *What a Black Man Saw in a White Man's Land* and *Footprints of a Black Man*. The latter book refers to his experiences while in Jerusalem. Dr. Brooks's contributions and influence in the African Methodist Episcopal Church are widely recognized to this day. (Calvert County Board of Education.)

Dadd

The Civil War had just ended when John Henry Locks was born to Benjamin and Eliza Locks on December 18, 1865. John was enrolled in the county school system at the age of six and continued his formal public education until he could go no farther. He then was tutored until age 19 by Pet Dorsey, ultimately becoming a teacher himself. He taught school for 35 years in the Calvert County public school system. (Mickey Ray.)

John Locks was a prominent figure in his community. He spoke throughout Maryland, instructing black voters how to mark their ballots, and was a member of the Galilean Fishermen, Masons, and Odd Fellows. Locks's interests included holding all-day community picnics and airplane exhibitions in the county. Prominent local people of both races attended his grand events. Locks was also the proprietor of the only black-owned general store at the time. (Mickey Ray.)

44

In 1920, the Calvert County Commissioners granted a sum of $5,000 to be used toward the construction of the Colored Industrial School (also known as the Central Colored High School). The Julius Rosenwald Foundation, named after the Sears and Roebuck president, also helped finance the construction of the school. The foundation, established in 1917, helped build schools throughout rural African American regions in 15 Southern states. (Linden House.)

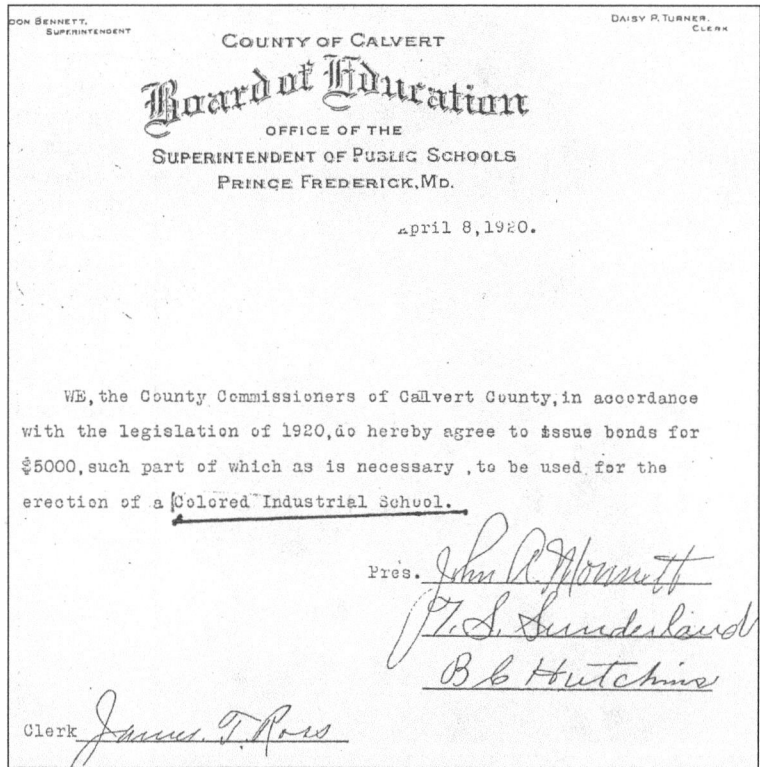

COUNTY OF CALVERT

Board of Education

OFFICE OF THE
SUPERINTENDENT OF PUBLIC SCHOOLS
PRINCE FREDERICK, MD.

April 8, 1920.

WE, the County Commissioners of Calvert County, in accordance with the legislation of 1920, do hereby agree to issue bonds for $5000, such part of which as is necessary, to be used for the erection of a Colored Industrial School.

Pres. John R. Mossutt

W. S. Sunderland

B C Hutchins

Clerk James T. Ross

The Old Wallville School, an 18-by-18-foot wood structure, is the oldest known African American one-room schoolhouse existing in Calvert County. A segregated school built in approximately 1867, it held 35 pupils in grades one through seven. The school was initially supported with funding from local African Americans. In 1934, a new one-room structure replaced the original building. Plans are under way to restore and preserve the school for future educational purposes. (Linden House.)

45

The young Lillian (née Ray) Roy spent her elementary school years in the Calvert County educational system. Believing she would receive a better education outside of the Calvert County school system at that time, she was sent to Baltimore to complete her secondary and high school studies. Receiving her Bachelor of Science degree from Morgan State College, she began teaching in the Montgomery County School system until her retirement in 1965. (Mickey Ray.)

Mount Hope Elementary teacher ? Handy would sometimes take her favorite students back to her hometown of Baltimore for the weekend. There the students would be exposed to some of the offerings of the city, such as the movies that these three young girls took in on this particular 1940s weekend. Pictured from left to right are students Peggy Jones, Alma Ray, and Delores Hayes. (Eloise Ray.)

Maryland High School Diploma

This is to certify that *Eloise Madeline Holland* has completed in a satisfactory manner at the

Central Colored High School, The General Course

of four years comprising at least the sixteen units prescribed by the State Board of Education for graduation from an Approved High School of the First Group and is accordingly awarded this

DIPLOMA

In Testimony whereof, the seal of the Board of Education of *Calvert* County and the signatures required by law are hereunto affixed this *sixth* day of *June 1938*

The Central Colored School, built in 1921, provided vocational and industrial education for African American children. The school provided a basic academic program for first through eleventh grades. The high school studies took place in the basement of the building while elementary teachings were provided on the upper floor. The last graduating class was in 1938, after which students attended Sampson Brooks High School. In 1938, Eloise Holland was in the last graduating class. (Eloise Ray.)

In 1993, Safe Harbor began occupying what used to be the Central Colored High School. Safe Harbor, supported by the Calvert County Health Department, is a place where women and children can seek shelter from domestic violence and spousal abuse. It provides medical services and counseling, as well as food and shelter. (Historic District Commission.)

Elizabeth Brown came from Philadelphia in 1930 to teach in Calvert County. Prior to equal pay for African American teachers, Brown's annual salary was $600, compared to her white counterparts with the same qualifications, who made $1,100. "I think there is a plan for people. I never intended to be a teacher, but it worked out that way," she said. Today Brown resides in Owings. (Madison Brown.)

This document, addressed to Elizabeth Brown from Thurgood Marshall, states that the Calvert County Board of Education refuses to pay equal salaries to African American teachers. Brown, then a teacher at Mount Hope School, had petitioned on behalf of African American teachers to have their salaries commensurate with their experience, much like their white colleagues. By 1939, the Calvert County Board of Education had agreed to pay African Americans equal salaries. (Madison Brown.)

At the rear of Brooks High School are, from left to right, Jane Reid, Doris Morsell, Phyliss Holland, Gladys Reid, and Carol Morsell. On this day in 1946, Reid graduated high school alongside 14 other students. She went on to get her teaching degree from Bennett College for Women, then returned to her alma mater to teach home economics from 1952 to 1966. (Beatrice Fletcher.)

Although he only attended school through the fourth grade, Jane (née Reid) Fletcher's father, Allnutt, recognized the importance of education. "We had to go to school rain or shine because he said he believed in education," Jane noted. "He said, 'You need to have some type of education to get along in this world.' And therefore he tried to see that we all got educated." (William Poe.)

Vivian (née Wheeler) Jones came from Pennsylvania in 1947 to teach in the Calvert County School system. After graduating from the Tuskegee Institute and a short stint teaching in Georgia, Jones began educating Calvert students at the Lusby School, a one-room schoolhouse with no facilities. She continued to teach in several county schools until 1966, when she was selected to be principal at the newly integrated Brooks Elementary School. She is pictured with her husband, Wesley, in the 1970s. (Jones family.)

Vivian (née Wheeler) Jones (second from right) is walking the campus at the Tuskegee Institute in Alabama with friend Ezelle Lanier (far right) in 1942. "I still value my wings I received at Tuskegee. My grandson who went to Tuskegee took them with him when he enrolled in the Aeronautical Engineering Program," she said. The other two students are unidentified. (Jones family.)

County commissioner Wilson Hamilton Parran stands in front of the barn in 2006 that his father used as a tenant farmer. The son of Roosevelt and Gonia (née Macgruder) Parran, Wilson was inspired by the powerful words of his father to continue his formal education upon graduating from Calvert High School. While he was in the eleventh grade, a construction worker who labored alongside Wilson's father during the tobacco off-season asked when he would be joining them in the construction trade. His father spoke up, "If he's gone to school for twelve years and he's gonna do the same thing I'm doing, then he's wasting his education." Wilson Parran received his master's degree from George Washington and became the first black president of the Calvert County Board of Commissioners to be reelected as president for a second term. In addition, he served as president of the Maryland Association of Boards of Education and as president of the Maryland State Board of Education. He became president of the Maryland Association of Counties in 2009. (William Poe.)

Macarthur Jones remembers that his father, Genious, continually aspired to better living conditions for his family. Hope for a better future came from the encouragement of his wife, Mary. Aside from being a tenant farmer, Genious Jones also had a well digging business. Although Macarthur experienced being a field hand on his father's farm, he sought higher education, attaining his master's degree from Bowie State University. Jones comments on how the ratio of African Americans has changed over the last few decades: "In 1975, I became the vice principal at Huntingtown Elementary, and I remember specifically at that time . . . the ratio was close to 49 percent minority, 51 percent Caucasian. When I came outta high school in 1961 the ratio was 51 percent minority, 49 percent Caucasian. And since 1975, the influx of population has been basically of the Caucasian race. . . . It resulted mainly from the fact that high school students of the black population, when they came outta high school, didn't care to stay here in the county . . . because they saw this as an agrarian society still. They went away to college, the military, or to Washington, D.C., went for the lights and opted not to come back." (William Poe.)

Bessie (née Jones) Moore was born in 1921 in Huntingtown. She received her Bachelor of Science degree from the State Teacher's College in Bowie, Maryland, in 1942. She also studied at Morgan College, the University of Maryland, and Bowie State University. Upon her graduation, she returned to Calvert County to teach in the public school system, retiring in 1974. Moore still resides on the family farm purchased by her grandfather Joe Jones. (Bessie Moore.)

Ilean Ray, daughter of Clyde and Pearl Jones, attended Bowie State College from 1952 to 1954. Upon graduation, she moved to Baltimore and taught elementary school in Prince George's County until 1988. "I retired to take care of my mom, who had diabetes," Ray said. Ray returned to her parents' farm in Calvert County, where she currently resides. (Ilean Ray.)

ELEMENTARY SCHOOL REPORT CARD

SCHOOL Dares
PUPIL Leon Holland
GRADE 5th   YEAR 19 46 19 47
TEACHER Lauren Alston

SYSTEM OF GRADING

A-SUPERIOR WORK; B-GOOD, ABOVE AVERAGE; C-AVERAGE
D-BELOW AVERAGE
E-FAILURE.

PRINCIPAL E. W. Cordery

Wilson Leon Holland's fifth-grade report card from Dares Elementary School reflects his early academic achievements. According to Warrick Hill, Holland's seventh-grade teacher at Brooks High School, he was a quiet, well-mannered honor student. In 1951, Holland, then in tenth grade, transferred to Pine Forge Academy in Pennsylvania. Pine Forge Academy was one of the oldest African American boarding schools in the nation. (Marsha Plater.)

Wilson Leon Holland stands at the podium on the grounds of Pine Forge Academy delivering his graduation speech. Holland included the poem "Be Strong," by Maltbie Davenport Babcock, in his speech. He was the senior class president and sang baritone in the school's traveling choir. He graduated from the academy in 1954. (Marsha Plater.)

On this spring day in 1955, friends pose on the steps at Brooks High School. From left to right are Gertrude Holland, Dorothy Wallace, Phyllis Greene, Cleo Gray, and Ella Mackall. The girls were enjoying their freshmen year at school. "All of us were in the chorus together. Phyllis and I were in the Drama Club, and Ella was a cheerleader in the band," Cleo (née Gray) Brown remembers. (Brown family.)

At the age of 15, Allan Brown (pictured in 1957) began playing the trombone. "I was in the Brooks High School original band," he remembers. "Buddy Carter was in there with me. We both played trombone. I watched Jimmy and Tommy Dorsey on the television one night, and after that I wanted to play." His parents paid on credit $15 a month for the instrument. (Brown family.)

Blanche (née Jones) Harris and James Hutchins were two of the first four students to integrate the all-white Calvert Senior High School in 1963. Maryland had already passed its integration law guaranteeing equal education but had not yet proceeded with the process. She remembers, "Some of the students would walk on the other side of the building's sidewalks instead of passing by you on the same side." She continues, "I was befriended by some and ignored by others. Over the next 30 years, I had several people call me about the class reunion and apologized at that time for the treatment we received from fellow students." Jones has been married for 41 years and has three children and two grandchildren. Hutchins currently lives in St. Mary's County. (Both, Calvert High School yearbook.)

Four

COMMUNITY

Oliver Foote was a tenant farmer and oysterman. He began catching oysters with his father in the Patuxent River when he was 13 years old. He remembered "catching 30 and 40 bushels of oyster a day. I sold oysters from 15, 25¢ a bushel, and when the war broke out, we start getting about 45¢ a bushel." Foote served in the army in 1943. When asked during an interview shortly before his passing, "How do you think things have gotten better for you or have they and, 40 years later (after the civil rights movement), what are your thoughts?" Foote responded, "For some, like I told you, for some it has. For Washington, some things have changed a whole lot. Because it was Washington that got burn out and (if) it hadn't a been burn out in Washington things would, nothing had a happened. But it was . . . Washington that burn out, and they was scared they gonna burn the White House out, so therefore, they did something in Washington. And now . . . only time that they can do anything in Washington they got to tear down something to do something there." (William Poe.)

Pictured in his parents' home in Port Republic is Andre Jones, a local music sensation. A gifted musician, singer, and songwriter, Jones (pictured at the age of 8), began showcasing his talents at the age of 3. Son of Francis and Gladys Jones, Andre has performed on different occasions for Maryland governor Martin O'Malley and Congressman Steny Hoyer, as well as for many other special events. In 2007, Jones was a two-time Apollo Theater winner. (William Poe: 2006.)

The daughter of sharecropping/ tenant farming parents, Mary Holland (pictured in the 1940s) became a tenant farmer herself, along with her husband, Smitty Holland. "It was hard work but not to me. I enjoyed it," she said. After attending St. Paul Practical Nursing School in Baltimore, Holland returned home to Calvert County and began farming and raising a family. She later went to work with the Department of the Navy, retiring in 1991. (Mary Holland.)

This postcard, dated May 5, 1948, shows, from left to right, Gladys Ozella "Doris" Morsell, John Jackson, and Malinda Brooks. The photograph was probably taken in the apartment of Jackson and his wife, Hattie (née Brooks), in Washington, D.C. Jackson, originally from King William County, Virginia, served in World War II as a baker. Brooks, the mother of six children, went back to school after her children were grown and received her degree in business at the age of 63. (Marsha Plater.)

Ruth Smith of Huntingtown is shown being honored by the St. Mary's Rotary Club in 1982. Smith was an employee of the Warren Denton Oyster Company in Broomes Island for nearly 30 years. She became the U.S. National Oyster Shucking Champion after defeating her brother, Cornelius Mackall, at the St. Mary's County Oyster Festival. She was a three-time national champion and went on to compete in the International Oyster Shucking Championship in Gelway, Ireland, representing the United States. (Ruth Smith.)

Enoch Columbus Tyler, born in 1910 in Hunting Creek, was the son of sharecropping parents, Sam and Sarah Tyler. One of 18 children, he was formally educated for only a short time in elementary school. Like most children of sharecroppers, Tyler had to sacrifice his schooling in order to help his family with the farming labor. "I never had more than 100 days of school, but I could do more than most men could who were educated," Enoch said. As a young boy, Enoch saw the first automobile drive into Calvert County. Pictured in the early 1920s are (first row) unidentified, Ben Tyler, Harriet Tyler, and unidentified; (second row) unidentified, Sarah Tyler (mother) holding Erna Tyler, Enoch Tyler, and unidentified. Off to the right is a chicken coop. (Mary Holland.)

At the age of 18, Enoch Tyler married Martha Elizabeth Freeland. They had three children: Enoch Jr., Mary, and Evelyn. Like many African Americans of Calvert County at that time, Enoch became a sharecropper (as well as a tenant farmer). Often faced with unfavorable living conditions, such as tiny uninsulated houses without running water or electricity, sharecroppers and tenant farmers frequently worked from sunrise to sunset and sometimes longer, working by the light of a lantern in their barns. While he was tenant farming for one landowner in the early 1930s, Enoch's daughter Evelyn, at the age of five, died of typhoid fever. The entire family had contracted the deadly disease when the landowner refused to dig a new well for the Tylers. The Tyler family had been using a spring as their source of water, which became blocked by a felled poplar tree, eventually contaminating the water supply. (Both, Mary Holland: early 1950s.)

Enoch Tyler, at the age of 96, sits in his apartment at the Calvert Pines Senior Center during a 2006 interview with William Poe. The interview was part of an oral history project that documented the lives of tenant farmers of Calvert County. Known as one of the best tobacco growers of his time, Tyler had a crop of tobacco that brought in $12,000 at the tobacco market in the late 1940s, an unheard of amount for that time. Tyler passed away on February 22, 2007, at the age of 97. The "I Am Somebody" Scholarship Fund, which helps descendants of tenant farmers and sharecroppers further their education, was created in honor of Enoch Tyler. (William Poe.)

John Samuel Tyler stands next to his yoke of steer in the early 1920s. Before machinery became standard practice for farming use, farmers often relied on steer, horses, and mules to do most of the field work, such as cultivating, plowing, and hauling. Aside from being a sharecropper, John Tyler was also a horse breeder, and he often traveling to adjoining counties to breed horses for other farmers. His mother, Harriet Holland, was an ex-slave when he was born. His father was white, possibly her former slave owner. He took the name of his stepfather, Jim Tyler, who was also an ex-slave from the Deep South. (Mary Holland.)

Members of Plum Point and Patuxent United Methodist Churches joined together to form the Huntingtown Charge Softball Team. The team participated in the Men's Christian League, along with other local church organizations. This photograph from the early 1980s was taken at Hallowing Point Park. From left to right are (first row) Hamilton Parran Jr., Alvin Wills, Therman Gray II, Joseph Parran Sr., Joseph Parran II, Frank Cook, and Shawn Brooks Sr. (second row) Dana Jones, Vada Brooks, Therman Gray Sr., Vaughn Reid Sr., Paul Jones, Ronald Jones Sr., Cepada Long, and Macarthur Jones; (third row) Derrick Brown, Louis Long, Michael Watts, George Jones, Tyronne Jones, and Ralph Parran Sr. (Parran family.)

Russell Mackall was born in Prince Frederick in 1937. He is a third-generation tobacco farmer. Mackall refused to take the "tobacco buyout" plan offered by the Maryland government, an incentive that pays farmers to not grow tobacco for a 10-year period. He continues to raise between four and eight acres of tobacco annually on his own land and is possibly the last African American tobacco farmer in Calvert County. Mackall's fate as a tobacco grower is unknown. In the photograph below, Mackall uses a stripping machine. Most farmers did not have the luxury of this type of machine. This reduces Mackall's need for labor. (Both, William Poe.)

After completing her master's degree program at George Washington University, Ruth Reid began teaching at W. S. Brooks High School. Appointed as Calvert's first Pupil Personnel Worker in 1964, Reid worked closely with troubled youth and their families. Reid eventually went on to teach as a professor at Bowie State College from 1971 to 1982. She continues to be a prominent leader in Calvert County's civic affairs with many honors to her name.

James Jones, the son of Elizabeth and Phillip, was taught by his parents to read and write. Jones apparently had a contagious disease, preventing him from being able to attend school. This 1950s photograph of him was taken in Baltimore, where Jones eventually moved. He was a television and radio repairman with a repair shop located behind his house. (Timothy Jones.)

Lena and William Jones pose for a 1930s photograph outside of their tenant home in Huntingtown. The Joneses, who had 12 children, worked as tenant farmers most of their lives. Tenant farming and sharecropping were widespread in Calvert County for most of the 20th century. Tenant farmers would live in modest housing on a landowner's property and work the land in exchange for housing and 50 percent of the proceeds from the sale of their tobacco crops. (Dorothy Jones.)

In 1959, Allan Brown stands next to his best friend's bike. His brother Steven stands behind him. Brown and Buddy Carter were inseparable since ninth grade at Brooks High School. "He had only owned the bike for about one week when he left it with me. He went to Salisbury with the 4-H Club and told me to learn how to ride it while he was gone," Brown recalls. They remain friends to this day. (Brown family.)

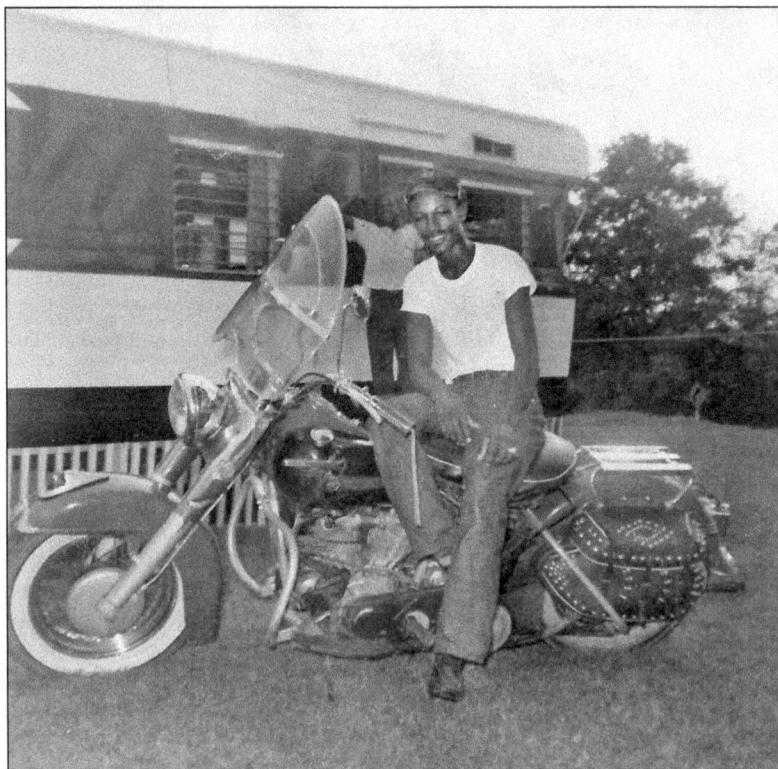

George Henry Evans, shown in 1993, was sometimes referred to as "the Mayor" of Dunkirk. Deeply devoted to Peter's United Methodist Church, Evans was superintendent of Sunday school and president of the Methodist Men, as well as chairman of trustee and custodian of the church. He became a 33rd-degree Mason in 1951. His occupations included farmer, carpenter, and animal trainer. Evans fathered a total of 17 children. His marriage to Mabel Randall lasted 62 years. (Evans family.)

Homegoing Celebration

for

George Henry Evans

December 12, 1907 — March 24, 1993

Sunday, March 28, 1993

Family Hour: 10:30 A.M. — Funeral: 11:00 A.M.

Peter's United Methodist Church

Dunkirk, Calvert County, Maryland

BROTHER IRVING BEVERLY, *Officiating*

REVEREND JOHNNY WASHINGTON, *Pastor*

George Henry Evans (who went by "Henry") and his wife, Mabel (née Randall), were the parents of nine boys and four girls. This photograph of the Evans brothers was taken in 1960 at the home of Henry and Mabel. Pictured from left to right are (first row) Richard and Warren; (second row) Leroy, Herbert, and Daniel; (third row) Levi, Ernest, Robert, and Joseph. There are seven surviving brothers. (Joseph Evans.)

WARFIELD & ROHR COMPANY

MANUFACTURERS & JOBBERS OF

UNDERTAKERS' SUPPLIES

323-325 NORTH CALVERT ST.

BALTIMORE, MD. Aug.6,1925

No 3050

RECD.

DATE OF ORDER

SALESMAN

VIA

SOLD TO Wm.H.Smothers
Olivet Md

TERMS: 5% 30 Days Net 60

QUANTITY	DESCRIPTION	STYLE	PRICE	AMOUNT	TOTAL
2	6/0	56		38 00	
2	Boxes			16 00	

William Smothers was a prominent figure in his time. One of his occupations was undertaker. This 1925 document is a receipt for goods purchased from the Warfield and Rohr Company. Englis Gray, the great-grandson of Smothers, recalls, "The coffins were shipped from Baltimore on a steamboat, and they would go by rowboat to pick up the coffins. My grandmother would help put the linings and the handles on the caskets." (Gray family.)

HARRISON W. VICKERS, JR.
COMMISSIONER

STATE OF MARYLAND
CONSERVATION DEPARTMENT
512 MUNSEY BUILDING
BALTIMORE, MD.

April 2, 1923.

Mr. Wm. H. Smothers,
Solomons, Md.

Dear Sir :-

We are enclosing herewith your permanent lease for 2 acres of oyster ground, to replace the temporary lease sent you April 30, 1921.

Please execute this lease by signing your name on the line above the word LESSEE and have a witness sign on the line below Mr. Earle's name. Then return the lease to this office to be signed and recorded. We are enclosing an envelope for this purpose.

You will notice that your lease is for 1 acre more than you originally applied for, and have been paying rent on, so we are enclosing a bill for the difference. As your rent falls due the 30th of this month, we are including another year's rent on the bill.

When you return your lease to be recorded, please also let us have your check in settlement of this bill.

Very truly yours,

H.B.Johnson
Chief Clerk

J:P
Enc.

William Smothers was also an oysterman. Many African Americans in the southern part of the county made their living on the water. "They depended on the water," said his granddaughter, Dorothy Gray. Gray remembers accompanying her grandfather on his boat as a young girl. Smothers, who had a home in the Mill Creek area, oystered until his passing in 1926. (Gray family: 1923.)

Commissioner Wilson Parran describes his father, Roosevelt (pictured): "My father was a hard worker, he didn't really say a lot, he was kind of a quiet person. . . . That profound statement he made when I was growing up, still sticks with me about, you gotta do something to better yourself in life. He knew that there was something better than just working construction in off-season and sharecropping the rest of the time." (Wilson Parran.)

Commissioner Wilson Parran remembers his mother, Gonia (Macgruder): "She was a very religious person; she was optimistic, always optimistic. I don't think she's ever been negative about anything. Always made the best out of whatever situation she was in, and that helped. That rubbed off on me, rubbed off on some of the others, my brothers and sisters." (Wilson Parran.)

George Jones (left) owned a large parcel of land in Huntingtown next to his brother Joseph's farm. Jones and his wife, Annie (née Gross, below), raised tobacco and corn, as did most other local farmers in Calvert County at that time. The tobacco grown and cured in Calvert County had to be shipped in a hogshead to Baltimore, where the tobacco market was located at the time. The farmers often had to wait until the following year to receive the monies due them from the sale of their crops. Upon the death of her husband, Annie Jones moved to Baltimore, where she practiced nursing. (Both, Dorothy Jones: in the early 1900s.)

By the early 1940s, Clyde Jones, a tobacco farmer in Sunderland, owned approximately 175 acres. He managed to save enough money from hauling tobacco to Baltimore for other farmers and operating a school bus business to purchase and add 150 acres to his initial 25-acre farm. Pictured in the 1940s from left to right are Ernest Kent, district extension agent Martin Bailey, and Clyde Jones. (Ilean Ray.)

Tobacco farmer Clyde Jones and others are inspecting the flower of his tobacco plants. The flowers would be topped, or removed, before the plants were cut and hung in the barns to cure. Jones's farming operation, in conjunction with his school bus contracting business, sawmill production, and hauling services, grossed $30,000 a year in the early 1940s. Pictured from left to right are Ernest Kent, two unidentified, Clyde Jones, district agent Martin Bailey, John Jennings, and Gaines Scott. (Ilean Ray.)

Clyde and Pearl Jones are in their tobacco barn inspecting the previous year's crop. Jones eventually had two tenant families living on his farm to help with the 40 acres of tobacco he was raising. His annual tobacco yield averaged 30,000 pounds, grossing $12,000 for Jones and his tenants. (Ilean Ray.)

A young farm hand passes down cured tobacco to Clyde Jones in the 1940s. The next step would be the stripping process, where workers would remove the leaves from the tobacco stalk and categorize them. Their location on the stalk would determine the quality of the leaf and, in turn, determined the market value of the tobacco. (Ilean Ray.)

Pearl Jones is shown here with 4-H member John Jennings in her kitchen preparing to make butter. In addition to raising their five children, Jones also worked the tobacco fields with her husband, tended a garden, and milked the family cow. They rarely had to purchase goods from local general stores. (Ilean Ray.)

Kinsey Jones is pictured in the 1950s in front of his truck with one of his hunting dogs. Jones and his brother Jimmy had several beagles they used during squirrel and raccoon season. When asked if he ever hunted with his father and uncle, Timothy Jones replied, "No, they got up way before sun up to go hunting. Everything was done early in the morning." (Timothy Jones.)

Tom and his younger brother Tim are pictured on their family's farm in Dunkirk in 1955. Their father, Kinsey Jones, was a tobacco farmer most of his life. The farm was approximately 13 acres and had been in the family since before the dawn of the 19th century. Tim Jones remembers, "Farming was hard work, but at least it was honest work. And it actually was fun because we all came together and helped one another." (Timothy Jones.)

Aileen Stamper came to Calvert County to teach in 1940. Her career began at W. S. Brooks High School, and she accepted the position of principal for the 1943–1944 school year. Recognized for her unwavering commitment to education, Stamper was also associated with many local civic groups and organizations. After working for 38 years in the Calvert County school system, Stamper retired in 1978. She passed away in 2004. (Paige Jones.)

A Celebration of Life

Sunrise
March 15, 1918

Sunset
April 18, 2004

Ailene Lois Stamper

May the service I gave speak for me
11:00 a.m.
Plum Point United Methodist Church
1800 Pinnett Road
Huntingtown, Maryland

Reverend Tunde E.O. Davies, Pastor Officiating

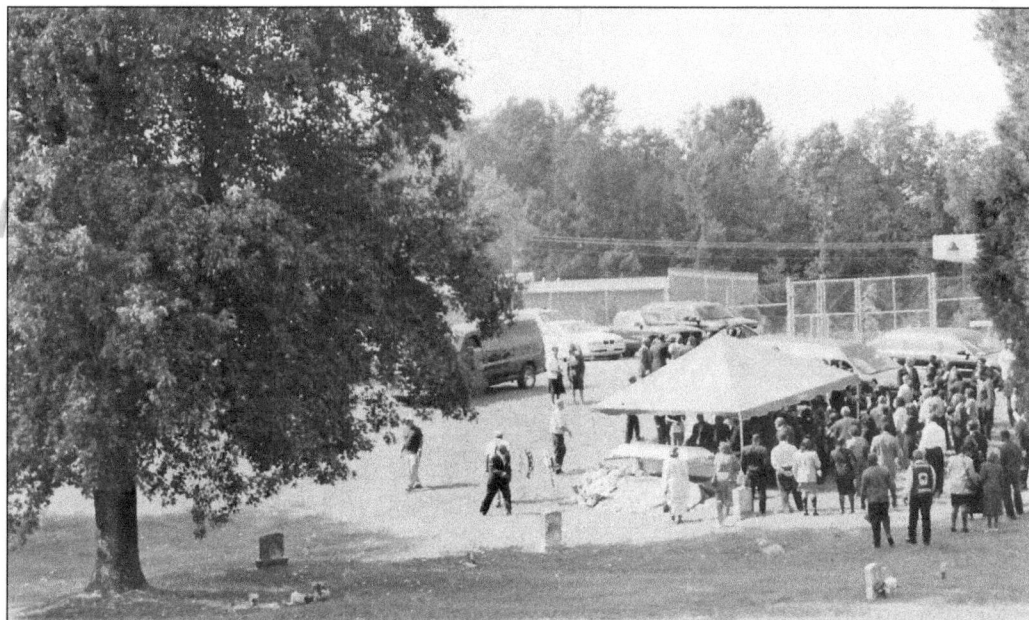

Helen Gray had been affectionately known throughout the Calvert community as "Fannie." She made her living as a domestic worker as well as a farmer. Although she retired from tobacco farming in her 80s, Gray continued to plant a vegetable garden up until the time of her death. Born on July 10, 1913, Gray passed away on September 22, 2006, at the age of 93. She is buried at Mount Hope United Methodist Church in Sunderland. (William Poe.)

Rachel Chase was a prominent woman for her time. Pictured outside her home with son Thomas Gray (standing), Chase purchased this house in Huntingtown, along with approximately 179 acres, for $2,000 in 1891. Family members lived in the home until sometime in the 1960s. The house is currently abandoned and in disrepair. (Jones family: 1930s.)

Louise Jones, known around town as "Ms. Lou," was the daughter of Wesley and Rachel Chase. A significant figure in her own right, Jones (pictured in the 1930s) was an active leader in her community. A member of the NAACP in 1931, she also belonged to the Eastern Star, the counterpart to the Order of Masons. Jones was a foster parent as well as a Sunday school teacher at Patuxent United Methodist Church. (Jones family.)

Received of Rachel C. Chase Five hundred, sixty ($560) cash and note for Five hundred dollars ($500) in payment for Model 90 Touring car (Overland) July 5th 1919.

Arthur W. Dowell —

This promissory note shows Rachel Chase's purchase of a Model 90 Touring Overlander. She purchased the vehicle in 1919 for $1,060 from prominent local attorney Arthur Dowell. It was possibly a wedding gift for her daughter Louise, who had married Harrison Jones just weeks earlier. (Jones family.)

I Hereby Certify, That on this _21st_ _____ day of _May_ One Thousand, Nine Hundred and _Nineteen_ at _the Parsonage in Huntingtown_ _Mr. Harrison Jones_ and _Miss Louise Chase_ were by me united in Marriage in accordance with the License issued by the Clerk of the Circuit Court for _Calvert,_ County, in the State of Maryland.

_Rev. John C. ___
Huntingtown
(OFFICIAL CHARACTER.)

This Certificate is to be given to the Contracting Parties.

This marriage certificate from 1919 shows the union between Harrison Jones and Louise Chase shortly after Jones's enlistment in the army was complete. Jones's father, Joe, owned large acreages of land, as did Chase's mother, Rachel. The two farms were located in Huntingtown and were adjoined, and both families raised large amounts of tobacco and corn. Harrison and Louise's granddaughter Deborah Riley speculated that it could have been a marriage of convenience in order to join the two farms. (Jones family.)

Maryland, Sc.

The State of Maryland.

To all Persons to whom these Presents shall come Greeting:

KNOW YE, That the last Will and Testament of *Rachel A. Chase, late*

of CALVERT COUNTY, deceased, hath in due form of law been exhibited, proved and recorded in the office

of the REGISTER OF WILLS FOR CALVERT COUNTY, a copy of which is to these Presents annexed; and

administration of all the goods, chattels, and credits of the deceased is hereby granted and committed

unto *Louise Chase Jones,*

the Execut-*rix* by the said Will appointed.

Witness, *Elisha B. Howes* Esq., Chief Judge of the

ORPHANS' COURT OF CALVERT COUNTY, this *twenty-fourth*

day of *January,* in the year of our Lord nineteen

hundred and twenty-*thirty-three*

TEST:

Stewart C. Gibson
Register of Wills for Calvert County.

When Rachel Chase died in 1933, she had amassed a substantial amount of personal property, including her farm. Her daughter Louise was the executor of her will. She left her entire estate to her four daughters, to be divided equally. In 2004, descendants of Rachel Chase opened two steam trunks that had been stored away since her passing. In it were documents and photographs that dated back to the late 19th century. (Jones family.)

Mickey (née Locks) Ray stands with his mother, Lillian Locks (left), and grandmother Maggie (née Gantt) Locks in the late 1930s. Behind them is the general store Maggie and John Locks owned and operated in Huntingtown. At the time, the Locks family owned the only African American store in Calvert County. Maggie Locks often gave free bags of candy to children as they passed her store on their way to church. (Mickey Ray.)

Agusta "Gussie" Kent (left) is pictured with her daughter, Madora Kent, in front of the family's house in Huntingtown in the 1940s. "Gussie" as she was affectionately known, not only farmed tobacco with her husband, Daniel, but also was a midwife in the community. Daniel Kent was a farmer and local preacher. Madora Kent left for New York in her early 20s. (Cleo Brown.)

Daniel Kent married Agusta "Gussie" Kent in 1911. He was one of 16 children born to Benjamin and Rachel Kent Sr. Daniel Kent was a lay minister and would preach at various local churches. A member of the Grand United Order of Odd Fellows, he apparently was the bookkeeper for the organization. Ledgers with dues and other types of records kept by the family indicate this. (Carrie Bertha Jones.)

Seated on the lap of Agusta "Gussie" Kent is her son Daniel Webster Gayhart Kent. Her arm is draped over her older son, Philip Hammond. The girl to her right is believed to be Hattie (last name unknown). Philip would later be drafted into World War II. At the request of their father, Daniel, Gayhart, who was also drafted, was allowed to defer his military duty to help maintain the 275-acre farm. Gayhart was 94 years old in 2008 and had farmed his entire life. He still resides on the family farm. Gussie is about 22 years old in this 1915 photograph. She was considered to be the family historian who kept the photographs and documents. She also insisted that all of her children get an education. Because schools for African Americans only continued to a certain grade, Gussie arranged for her children to attend school in Baltimore. (Carrie Bertha Jones.)

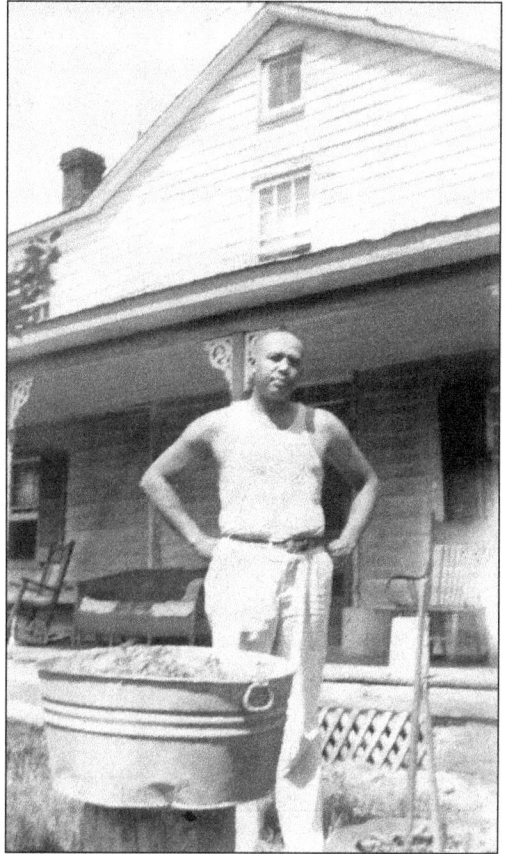

Eli and Sue Rice are seen in the 1940s at their home in Sunderland. The couple purchased 144 acres in 1902 from John and Jane Hutchins. According to Irving Cook, "When uncle Eli and Aunt Sue purchased the farm, they were asked how they were going to pay for it. 'Well, I want to know what the price is,' Uncle Eli replied. Uncle Eli had this money in a rubber band around his cuff of his pants and said, 'I gotta step into the next room.' He had enough one dollar bills down in his pants, in one pants leg to pay for the farm at that time. Aunt Sue said that the guy that was selling them the farm told her, 'If I had known that he had the money to pay for it, I would have never of sold it to him.' The sum was $1,500. (Both, Linden House.)

This photograph, taken at Sparrows Beach in the early 1960s, shows friends, from left to right, (first row) Agnes Jefferson, Gertrude Willett, Viola White, and Mary Watts; (second row) Gary Mason and George Buck. The picture was taken by Frances Hutchins. Hutchins recalls one of her visits to Sparrows Beach: "The last time I went there, we saw James Brown. My husband loved James Brown." (Hutchins family.)

Located in Benedict on the Patuxent River, Seagulls Beach was one of the area's segregated beaches for African Americans to enjoy. Frances Hutchins remembers Amos Young as the proprietor. The other two area beaches for African Americans were Sparrows and Carrs', located in Annapolis. Pictured in the 1960s from left to right are Pam Hutchins, George Hutchins, Ruth (née Greene) Bilal, Maurice Hutchins, and John (née Hutchins) Bilal. (Hutchins family.)

Born to tenant farming parents in 1923, Dorothy Jones began earning a living while still in grammar school. "And when I got about 10 years old, I used to work for the folks down there, Miss Prouty, from eight to one for a quarter and a leghorn chicken. . . . dust the floors upstairs and all that and clean up downstairs, you know, just wasn't no vacuum cleaner nothing then and wash the dishes up from the dinner," she said. She recalls stripping tobacco: "I used to take the children and carry 'em up barn, strip while my husband was working. I would take a . . . tin tub and carry it up, up to the barn in the car and uh, . . . bring the, take the baby out and put in a tub with a quilt you know, and set in the barn and I strip, I would strip by myself. My husband [was] working." (William Poe.)

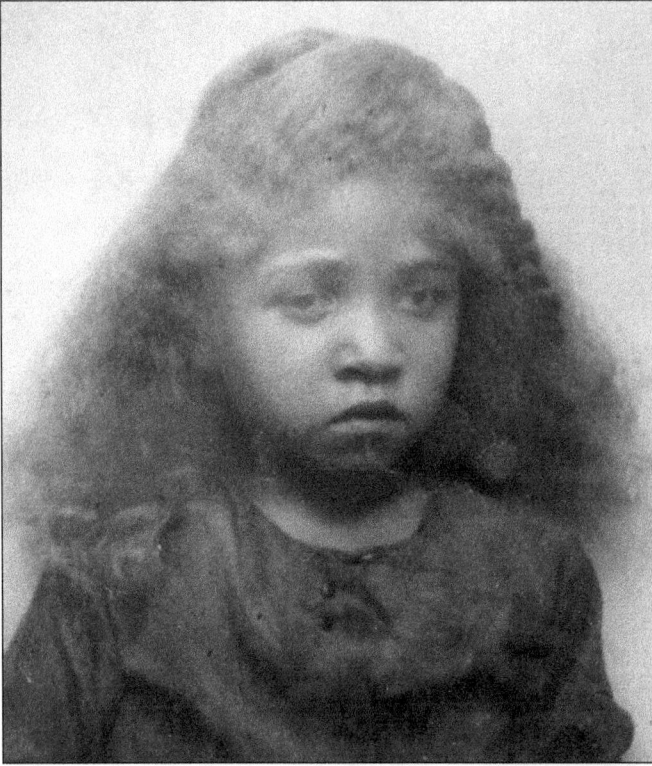

This photograph, taken in 1933, is of Mary Ruth Plater, the daughter of Earnest and Florence. Plater and her niece Doris became the first two African Americans employed by the Rod N' Reel, a local restaurant on the Chesapeake Bay. They continued working at the restaurant after their graduation from high school. Plater eventually married Clarence Coby and moved to Washington, D.C. She became the mother of twins in 1956, at the age of 31. (Marsha Plater.)

Florence (née Parker) Plater stands beside her home in 1956 with great-grandson Grafton. Plater's husband, Earnest, worked as a waiter in North Beach. She was a chef at a local bakery, Emma Ewalds. One of her favorite pastimes was sitting by the fence on Sunday afternoons and watching the cars pass by. Grafton was the son of Doris Plater and John Gilbert. (Marsha Plater.)

Born to Hezekiah and Ozella Brooks in 1885, Maurice Brooks was a highly skilled carpenter, learning the trade from his uncle, Ben Sewell. Brooks was a charter member of Victoria Lodge No. 71 Free and Accepted Masons, Prince Hall Affiliate. A builder of bridges and barns in the county, Brooks was sometimes compensated with hogs for his services. He married Agnes Coates in December 1909. Coates was born in 1892 to Samuel and Mary Coates. During their marriage, they had 14 children. Known to make her children's clothes, Agnes would sometimes take a pair of her husband's pants and make two pairs for her children. Their daughter Myrtle died tragically at the age of 15 in 1925. Unaware that gasoline had been mixed with the kerosene used for the family stove, Myrtle caught fire when she went to refuel the stove and the mixture exploded. (Marsha Plater.)

This photograph of Norman Gray was taken in a Baltimore studio in the 1940s. Gray, a local builder, built the St. Leonard Polling House as well as some of the local one-room schoolhouses. Gray's brother, Lindy, who was blind, operated a local gas station and relied on the honesty of his customers when dealing with paper money. (Gray family.)

Rosa Bourne was the first wife of Norman Gray. Bourne gave birth to nine children. She was from the Island Creek area and died during childbirth in 1925. She was in her mid-30s and is buried at Brooks Memorial in St. Leonard. (Gray family.)

In 1971, Englis Gray (third from left) received his pilot's license. Gray sometimes spoke at local schools during black history month. Gray rented this Aero Commando 112 and flew into the Chesapeake Ranch Estate Airport to talk to children at Appeal Elementary School about flying. Pictured from left to right in 1973 are Gray's father, David; Gray's mother, Dorothy; Gray; his young son Adam; and the principal of Appeal Elementary, Robert Conway. (Gray family.)

Dorothy (née Gray) Gomes is shown sitting on the lap of Santa Claus at the Sears Department store. During the holidays, the family would have to travel out of the county to share their Christmas list with Santa. "I don't remember a place in the county where we could take the children to see Santa Claus," Gomes's mother, Dorothy, recalls. Gomes was the fifth of five children. She was two at the time this 1959 photograph was taken. (Gray family.)

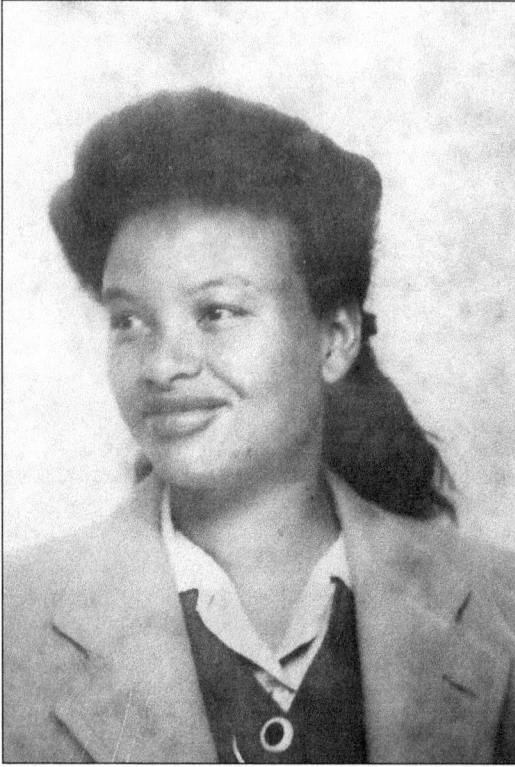

Born in Dares Beach in 1927 to Maurice and Agnes Brooks, Malinda Brooks married Roland Alexander Plater Sr. of Dunkirk in 1952. The service was held at the Mount Hope Parsonage in Sunderland. Throughout her life, Brooks held various occupations, including midwife. She was also a nanny for Supreme Court justice Barrett Prettyman. Involved with the local youth, Brooks started the first African American 4-H Club. The Platers had six children. (Marsha Plater.)

Daughters of Maurice and Agnes Brooks, Agnes (left) and Malinda pose at a Baltimore studio, probably in the late 1940s. Agnes gave birth to one son, Leon, but foster-parented an additional eight boys. She was recognized by Gov. Marvin Mandel for her dedication as a foster parent. Agnes died in 1978 from cancer; her younger sister, Malinda, died in 1993 from a brain tumor. (Marsha Plater.)

The inception for Marsha Plater's career began when she was completing the twelfth grade of high school at Takoma Academy. She says, "In twelfth grade, my girlfriend asked if I wanted a job working for her cousin who was a dentist. She said he needed a receptionist. Dr. Eugene Scott actually needed more than a receptionist. I would make the appointments, vacuum the office, clean the bathroom, pass the instruments, perform the sterilization, and collect the money. He said, 'You're really good at this. You have a good chair side manner and don't faint at the site of blood. You should become a hygienist.' In response, I said, 'This really looks easy—what you do. I would become a dentist!' " Dr. Marsha Plater graduated from the University of Maryland Dental School in 1983. She opened her practice in Prince Frederick in 1992. (Both, Marsha Plater.)

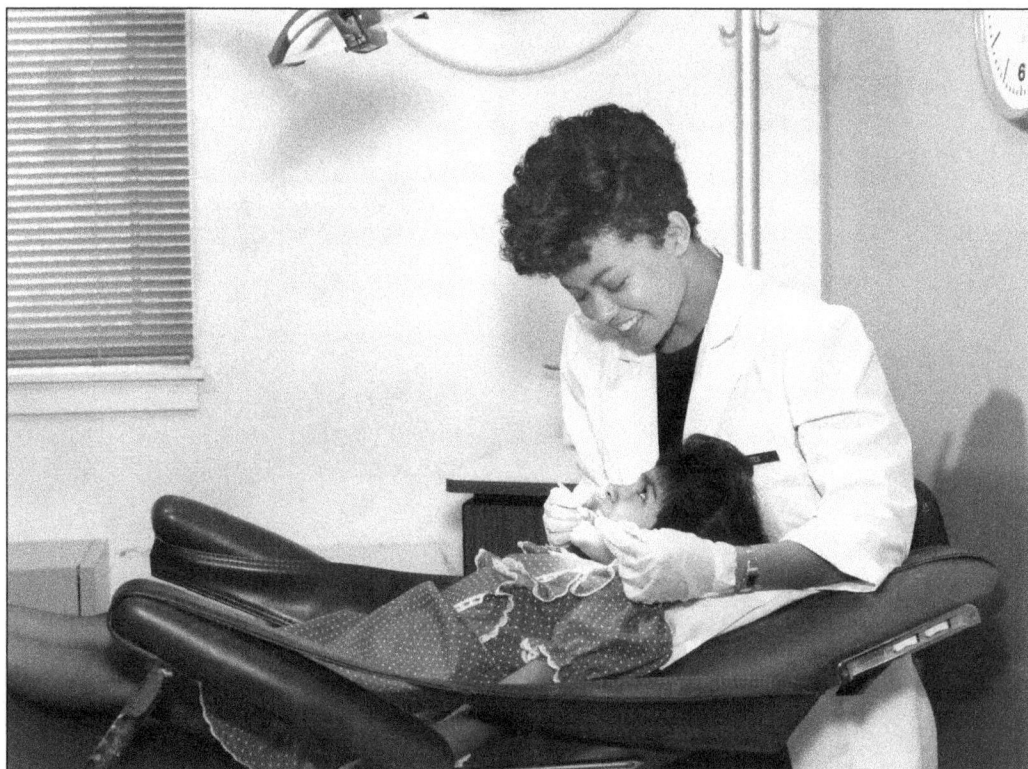

Because Calvert County was mainly an agricultural society, many bricklayers commuted to Washington, D.C., plying their trade. When the tobacco market began to diminish, farmers began selling off their land, which paved the way for the housing boom beginning in the late 1980s. Bricklayers, as well as other construction trades, no longer had to travel outside of the county to find work. Joseph Evans is humble yet proud of his work, saying, "What I like is everywhere around different neighborhoods, there is some house in there that I did the mason work on. And for myself, I know I did it, and it stands out for itself. I mean, I'm not bragging, but it ain't something I'm afraid to show anybody." Pictured at left, from bottom to top, are Reggie Evans, Warren Evans, Joseph Evans, and Russell Holland. The photograph below is of Joseph Evans on lunch break. (Both, William Poe.)

Joe Evans has been a bricklayer for nearly five decades. He attended masonry school for two years in Washington, D.C., before becoming a master bricklayer. Over the years, many family members have been employed by Evans. Having a reputation for being honest, Evans still conducts much of his business with a handshake agreement. "If you're going to do something, be honest about it," he says. "To me, I think you get along better. I've had people go bankrupt on me. You'd be surprised at the money I've lost. I could've retired. . . . But you know, I just try to be an honest person. The way my father taught me was just to be honest with people." The photograph below shows Evans on Easter Sunday in 2003 at Peters United Methodist Church. (Both, William Poe.)

JOSEPH EVANS & SON

P.O. Box 388 ~ Owings, MD 20826

410-741-5364

Mr __Billy Poe__   Date _11/12_ 20_03_

Address _____ Phone _____

City _____ State _____

DESCRIPTION OF WORK	LABOR TOTAL	TOTAL	
Put In Flue Jar in Chimney For store			
Cut out the Block wall on the Chimney			
Supply the Pipe For the Mail Box with 2 Pipe			
Supply the Materials For the Chimney			
Labor & Materials Cost		150	00
TOTALS			
LABOR TOTAL		150	00

By __Joseph Evans__

This handwritten bill is from Joseph Evans to the author in 2003. Joseph Evans and Son had just completed laying 37,000 brick on William Poe's house. Evans had just turned 71 years old and had no intention of retiring. "I'm not giving it up. I'll do it as long as I can do it," Evans remarked. His sentiment seems to reflect the work ethic of the community. (William Poe.)

Wilson and Agnes Holland are pictured in this studio photograph, probably taken in Baltimore in the 1940s. In 1951, the Hollands sent their only son, Leon, to Huntsville, Alabama, to attend Oakwood College. After the death of his wife in 1978, Wilson never remarried. He is 96 years old and still remains active in his church. (Marsha Plater.)

94

Eureka Lodge No. 36 (pictured above) was located in St. Leonard. It was the first African American Masonic Temple Lodge in Calvert County. The date of the lodge's origins is unknown but predates 1920. In 1920, some members of Eureka Lodge sought permission to create a new lodge in the neighboring Prince Frederick area for unspecified reasons, possibly for the convenience of members residing in the central part of the county. From this, Victoria Lodge No. 71 was chartered. (Victoria Lodge.)

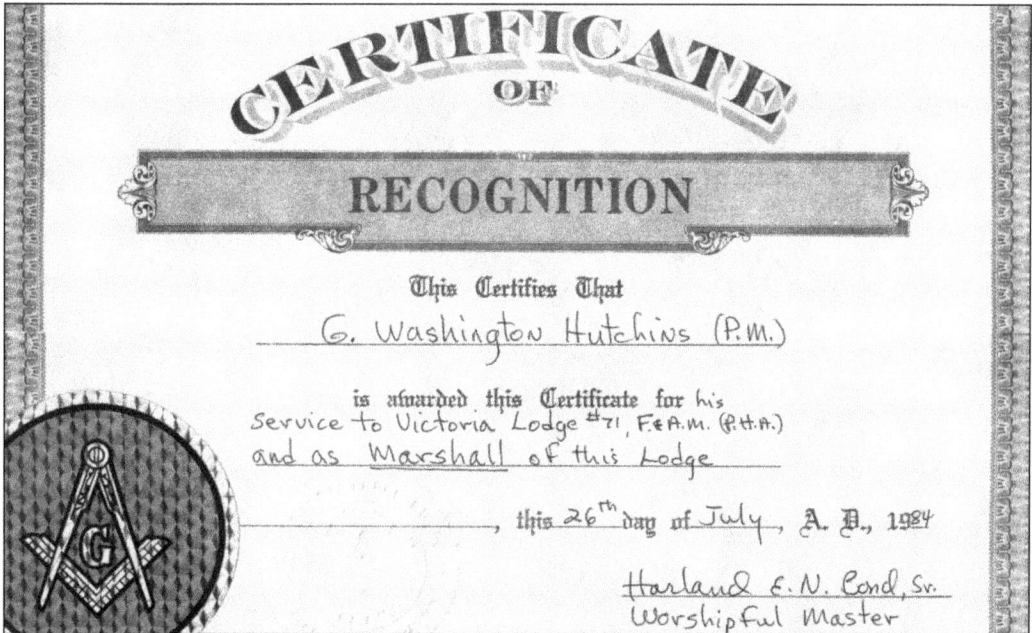

This 1984 certificate of recognition was presented to past master George Washington Hutchins of Victoria Lodge No. 71, F&AM in 1984. The charter members of Victoria Lodge No. 71 were James Brooks, John Scalyes, and Maurice Brooks. Victoria Lodge has continued to be a leader among organizations in Calvert County, making contributions to charitable causes as well as having many volunteer hours spent with local civic organizations. (Hutchins family.)

The Owings Eagles are posing for an early-1950s team photograph at Gray's Field in Owings. From left to right are (first row) unidentified, Bernard Rawlings, Judy Evans, Frances Wallace, Billy Spriggs, Taberius Reid, and John Jones; (second row) George Gray Sr., Marion Holland, Son Smith, Ellsworth Conte, William Jones, Bob Jones, Lawrence Gray, Hammy Wallace, Albert Gray Jr., and owner Albert Gray Sr. (Oscar Gray.)

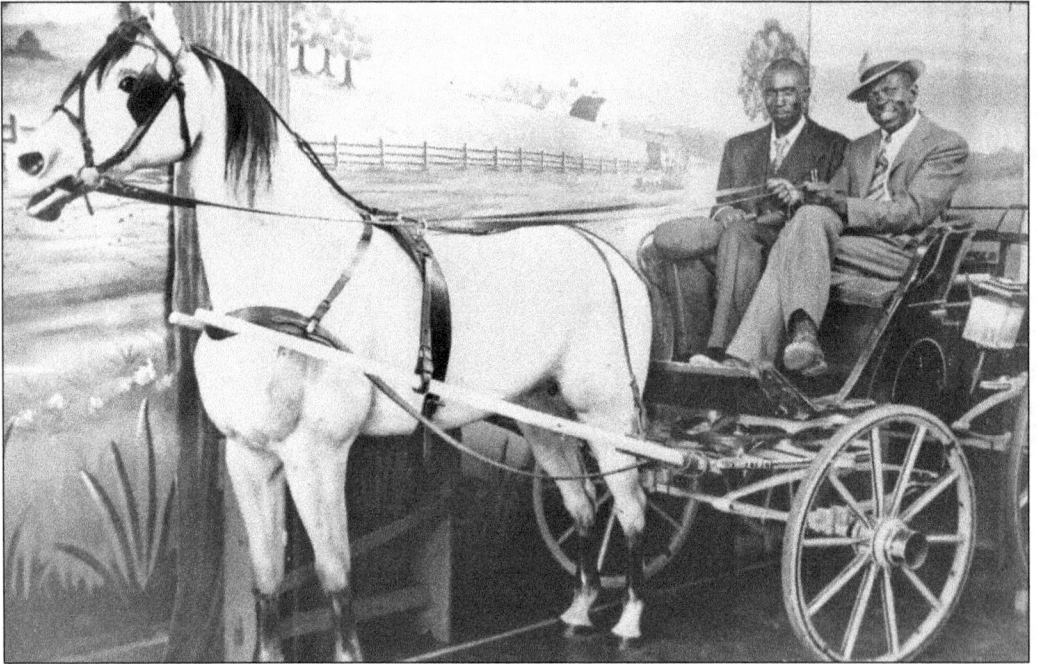

The owner of the Owings Eagles baseball team, Albert Gray Sr. (right), and Elijah Jacks pose in the 1940s atop this horse and carriage in a studio believed to be in Baltimore. Albert Gray purchased four acres of land in 1935 and built his home as well as Gray's Field, where the Owings Eagles played in the Negro League. Gray's Field was the first ball field in Calvert County to have lights installed for nighttime playing. (Oscar Gray.)

This 1950s picture of Maurice Brooks Sr. (seated) and Roland Plater Sr. was taken in the Dares Beach area. Plater was the son-in-law of Brooks. While Plater was a gas station attendant at Kenneth Ogden's Esso on Main Street in Prince Frederick, his future wife, Malinda, would have to park her bus around the back to make room for customers while she was visiting Roland. Maurice Brooks Sr. died in 1957. (Marsha Plater.)

SCHEDULE FOR HUNTINGTOWN CIRCUIT,

SOUTH BALTIMORE DISTRICT,

Washington Conference Methodist Episcopal Church,

1893 and 1894

REV. C. G. KEY, PRESIDING ELDER.

CHURCHES.	Schedule numbers (1893 May–Dec / 1894 Jan–April)
PATUXENT	1 6 1 2 1 7 4 1 5 1 7 1 4 5 1 9 1 8 4 1 9 1 11 5 12 1 1 4 3
BROWN'S	1 8 1 8 1 11 12 1 3 1 9 1 8 4 1 5 1 2 12 1 5 1 7 10 11 1 12 7
PLUM POINT	5 1 3 1 6 1 5 7 1 2 1 10 1 11 5 1 8 1 7 9 1 5 1 7 1 2 1 9
ST. EDMUND'S	9 1 10 1 5 1 9 6 1 4 1 6 1 9 11 1 12 1 9 6 1 10 1 6 1 7 1 5
MT. HOPE	11 1 4 1 12 1 11 10 1 11 1 5 1 6 3 1 5 1 6 8 1 11 1 1 1 10 1 10
ST. JOHN'S	12 1 12 1 9 1 10 3 1 8 1 2 1 12 5 1 7 1 10 12 1 12 1 1 9 1 12
COOPER'S	1 2 1 7 1 4 3 1 11 1 10 1 9 3 1 6 1 11 3 1 4 1 3 9 3 1 4 2
ST. PETER'S	1 11 1 8 1 3 8 1 10 1 4 1 11 7 1 12 1 5 11 1 11 1 8 10 11 1 6 11

1.—B. T. PERKINS, Preacher in Charge.

2. L. THOMAS,	5. S. F. MARSELL,	8. G. F. WATKINS,	11. J. T. JONES,
3. J. P. S. YOUNG,	6. DAVID EARLES, Sr.	9. D. EARLES, Jr	12. FRANK GILES.
4. J. W. BROWN,	7. J. B. MARSELL,	10. J. W. ROSS,	

— COLLECTIONS —

FIFTH SUNDAY IN JULY—FREEDMAN'S AID AND SOUTHERN EDUCATION. FIFTH SUNDAY IN OCTOBER—MISSIONARY. FIFTH SUNDAY IN DECEMBER—CONFERENCE CLAIMANTS. FIFTH SUNDAY IN APRIL—CHURCH EXTENSION.

N. B.—LOCAL PREACHERS AND EXHORTERS WILL TAKE THESE COLLECTIONS PROMPTLY. "GOD LOVES THE CHEERFUL GIVER."

This document shows the 1893–1894 annual schedule for the Huntingtown Circuit. This circuit was made up of eight churches in the vicinity, and the document lists the 12 pastors who presided over the churches on any given Sunday. Every Sunday, the churches on the circuit would rotate services, with four of them holding service. (Bessie Moore.)

Frances Hutchins (left) and Vera Evans enjoy a break at the Calvert Marine Museum. Hutchins began working at the museum in 1982. "The first four or five months, I was asked a lot of questions," she said. "You don't realize how much you learned until people start asking you questions and you're able to answer them." She retired from the Calvert Marine Museum in 1987. (Hutchins family.)

During the time of segregation, there was not a local Girl Scout troop that allowed African American children to participate. Frances Hutchins, with support from Florence Myers, began the first Girl Scout troop for them. Hutchins said, "They had four white Girl Scout troops, and Florence Myers had them. She told me to get the girls and meet her at my house. She was shocked. About 70 girls showed up." (Hutchins family.)

George Hutchins sits behind the wheel of his Chevrolet Impala sometime in the 1960s. The building to the left was the home of the Hutchins family. The building to the right is where Hutchins used to cut hair for his friends and clients. In 1946, he received his Maryland state license as a barber. After his retirement from the Naval Ordinance Lab in 1971, Hutchins went to work for the Calvert Cliffs Nuclear Power Plant. (Hutchins family.)

Joseph Jones and his second wife, Alice Ireland, are seen in their wedding photograph. Joseph Jones was born in 1853 to Priscilla Jones, a black woman, and Collin Chambers, a white man. The father of 18 children, Jones was a prosperous man, owning 350 acres of farmland, one of the largest farms owned by an African American in Calvert County at the time. He raised tobacco, corn, livestock, and poultry, as well as boasting one of the largest peach orchards in the area. He owned a Ford Model T, one of the first vehicles owned by a black man in the county. At the suggestion of his white counterparts, he withdrew his money from the bank just before the 1929 stock market crash, keeping his money in a cedar chest from that day forward. Many of his descendants live on land once owned by Joe Jones. (Dorothy Jones.)

There were several tobacco auction markets in the area that served the people of Calvert County. The Marlboro Tobacco Market, located in Prince George's County, was one of them. Landowners and tenant farmers would bring their cured tobacco to the warehouse hoping it would bring a better than decent price per pound. The major cigarette companies came annually to bid on Maryland's prized tobacco crop. These tobacco tickets of tenant farmers Arthur Stepney and Mabel Brown show the amount of pounds they, along with the owner-operator of the farm, brought to the market. It also shows the amount each burden brought in per pound, as well as the amount due to the operator, Wilson Dowell Jr., and the tenants of his farm. Fifty percent of the monies received went to the owner, and 50 percent went to the tenant farmers. (William Poe.)

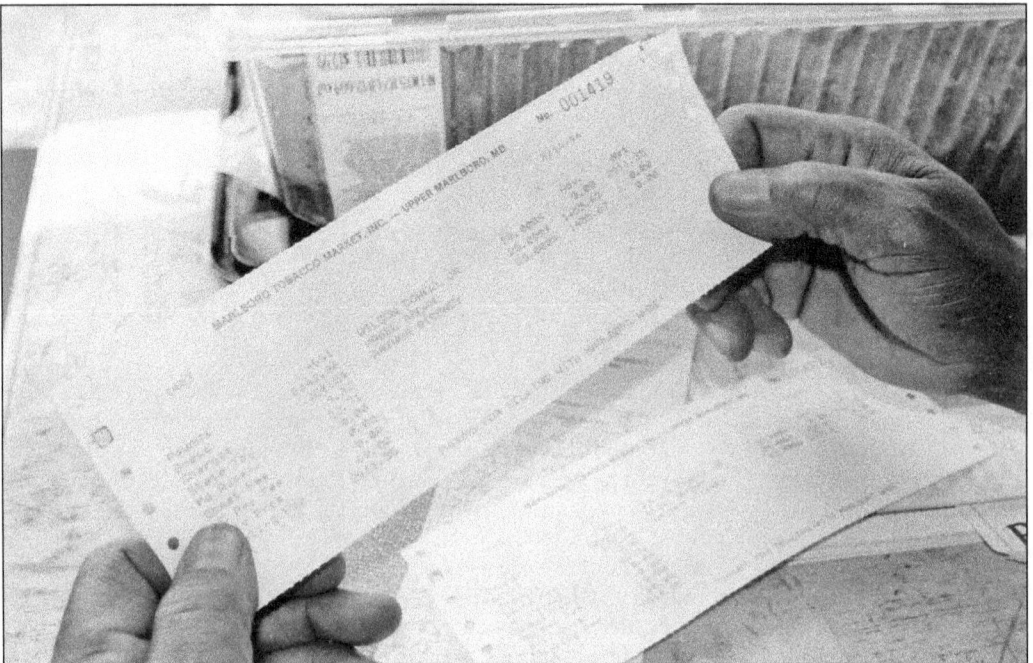

Marshall "Sharky" Randall (left) and his brother Luther are pictured in the Randall home during an interview in 2007. The Randalls are local grave diggers who have been servicing local churches and funeral homes for more than 40 years. It was with the passing of their older sister, who was 20 at the time, that they began opening graves. When asked why they got into their profession, Marshall referred to his sister's passing: "I wanted it done right, and I figured if I got into doing it, I could make sure it was done right. I want the proper size, the proper depth. When I walk away it's done right." Asked when they would retire, Luther said, "We keep saying we're gonna stop. As long as we have health and strength we try and do it." In the photograph below, Sharky completes the grave of Enoch Tyler. (Both, William Poe.)

In 2006, the community recognized Spencer Sewell for his contributions to the citizens of Calvert County. Sewell, owner of Sewell Funeral Home, became a licensed mortician in 1953. His grandfather Wilcis and his father, Pinkney, were also in the funeral business. (Sewell family.)

Spencer Sewell had his photograph taken in a Baltimore studio in his early 20s. Sewell became a school bus contractor in Calvert County in 1951. A year later, he received his mortician's license and helped with the family business. "Funerals back then cost 25, 50 dollars. Sometimes you even got paid with chickens, cows or hogs." He took over the family business in 1976. (Sewell family.)

Growing up on a farm and being a tenant farmer for much of his life, Irving Cook passes this advice on to the younger generation: "The first thing what I would tell the people . . . is young folks, you need to learn how to have manners and respect for everybody. Number two . . . you need to, in this day and time . . . seek the lord for direction. And he will direct your path." (William Poe.)

Rev. Benjamin Whiting and Essie Coates pose for a picture on their wedding day in the 1960s in Washington, D.C. This was the second marriage for Coates, who had previously been married for 52 years. She left Calvert County at the age of 18, moving to Washington, D.C., where she later became the owner of a beauty salon. As her health began to fail, she was taken care of by several of her nieces. (Marsha Plater.)

A photograph believed to be dated in 1915 is of the newly built Young's Methodist Church in Huntingtown. The church shown in this photograph was completed in 1912 and was named after the Reverend Alfred Young. Young was the pastor in charge while the new church was being built. A fire around 1910 had destroyed the old church, which was known on the Huntingtown Charge as Brown's Chapel. The Huntingtown Charge, which was established in 1875, consisted of eight churches: Patuxent, Peters, Mount Hope, Coopers, Plum Point, Browns, St. Edmonds, and St. Johns. The Freedmen's Aid Society may have been instrumental in building Young's Methodist Church. It is currently the worship site of the Calvert Christian Fellowship, Church of God of Prophecy. The man in the photograph is unidentified but may be Rev. Alfred Young. (Viola Kent.)

The Methodist Men of Plum Point and Patuxent United Methodist Church perform at a 2007 Songfeast program. The Songfeasts are held throughout the local African American churches and feature men's and women's choirs from various churches in the county, as well as performing groups from afar. This particular program was held at Patuxent United Methodist Church. Officiating minister of both churches is Rev. Tunde E. O. Davies. (Both, William Poe.)

George Washington Hutchins grew up in the southern part of the county in Dowell. Many of the men worked the local waterways for a living. Hutchins's father, Alexander Butler, transported goods such as timber and canned tomatoes to local ports along the Patuxent River and Chesapeake Bay. Hutchins, a recreational fisherman, was employed at the Naval Ordinance Laboratory Technical Facility in Solomons. He retired in 1971. (Hutchins family.)

Sisters Helen (née Hicks) Gray (left) and Hilda (née Hicks) Reid are pictured in the 1940s in front of one of the homes Gray lived in as a tenant farmer. She talks about farm life: "If you go out here and you raise your garden, you got your hog, you got your chicken, you got your milk cow, you got your eggs and things, and if you ain't too lazy, put up fruit, and make jelly, you can provide." (Gray family.)

Men were not the only tenant farmers. Women like Helen Gray also tended the fields, growing crops of tobacco and corn for landowners. Gray was born in 1913. Her work ethic began to take root at the age of five when she would help her father "drop tobacco plants" on freshly plowed mounds of soil. She began "working out" at age nine, scrubbing floors and doing dishes for a Miss Grace, a white lady who lived in the area. Working as a tenant farmer until she was in her late 80s, Gray also did domestic work during farming's off-season. She typically would slaughter two hogs every November in order to make homemade sausage and scrapple. Most farm families lived off the land and also owned livestock. When asked what type of advice she could pass along to the younger generations, Gray replied, "It not too much you can tell 'em, I said, but like you all think that you can live in this world and do anything you want and get by but you must listen to somebody." (William Poe.)

Raised by his grandparents John and Florence Gross, Ernest Evans was known affectionately throughout the community by his nickname, "Jake." He attended Peter's United Methodist Church in Chaney as a young boy, and his commitment to serve the Lord continued throughout his life. Until his death in 2007, Evan's distinct bass vocals supported three local church choirs. Late in his life, he became a devoted member of Patuxent United Methodist Church. He is buried at the church's cemetery. (William Poe.)

Eloise Ray recalls her father, Marion's, words of wisdom: "He brought us up all the time to be honest. He said if you ever get hungry and don't have nothing to eat, don't ever take nothing. You go and ask somebody can you scrub their floor if you didn't get no more than a quarter rather than take something." (William Poe.)

In their home in the 1960s, Frances (née Stewart) and her husband, John Albert King, pose for a family photograph. The Kings had 13 children. Their daughter Frances recalls, "Daddy was a farmer. Mom didn't farm; she was always at home raising the family, and we had to eat three meals each day, breakfast, dinner, and supper. They were the two most lovely people I know." (Hutchins family.)

Standing outside the Calvert County Courthouse in 1987 are bailiffs, from left to right, Ralph Hutchins, Thomas Weems, Frances Hutchins, and Bill ?. Frances Hutchins began working as a bailiff for the circuit court in 1987. She retired in 2000 because of her husband's illness. After his passing in 2001, she returned as a bailiff until her retirement. (Hutchins family.)

The first of several in the family to bear the name, Queenie Coates married Clarence Coore in 1919. The daughter of Samuel and Mary Coates, Queenie (pictured here in the 1930s) and her husband left for New York, where she was employed as an office worker. She would send clothes home to her family in Calvert County shipped in barrels by way of train or steamship. The couple had no children. (Marsha Plater.)

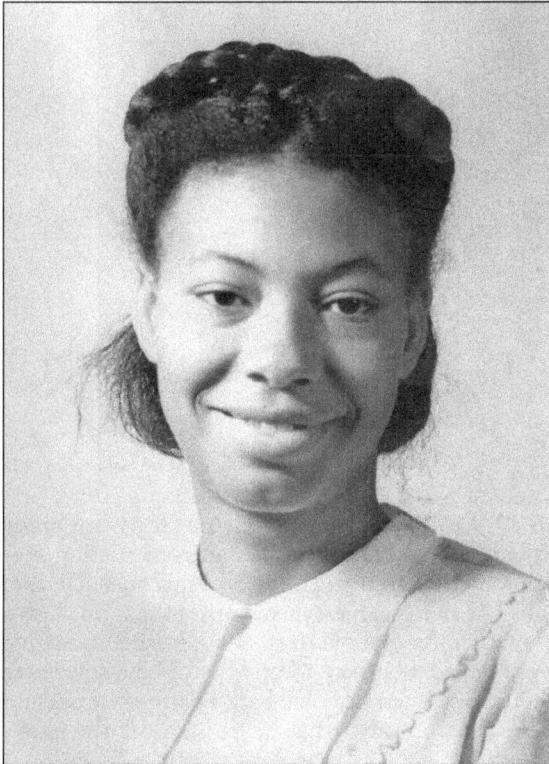

Queenie Brooks, seen in the 1940s, was the youngest daughter of Maurice and Agnes Brooks. After completing her education at Brooks High, Brooks was hired as a nanny at the home of a local white family. Eventually, she went to Washington, D.C., where she lived with her sister Hattie. She took the name Nolan after her first marriage and later Scarborough with her second husband. Between both unions, Brooks had three children. (Marsha Plater.)

George Henry "Broome" Harrod was born in 1919 in Plum Point. A tenant farmer for many years, he would earn additional income for his family by working on different construction sites as a block layer. Harrod hunted as a young man, sometimes selling the pelts of raccoons. Geneva Greene became his bride in 1938. Harrod recalls one of his earliest memories of the farm: "I was around 11, 12 years old, worked horses. My stepfather, he told me to go down to the house one day and had the horse hooked up to a thing you called a border . . . and he told me stay there and watch the horse until he go down to the house but when he come back I done went out and take the horse, pulled up and made two or three rows. . . . after that he let me work the horse, yeah." (William Poe.)

This picture of George Harrod and his family was taken in the early 1990s. From left to right are (first row) Charles, mother Geneva, father George, and Arlene; (second row) Carlene, Almous, Darlene, Harry, and Marion. (Darlene Harrod.)

On this particular day in 1962, Mount Harmony Elementary School hosted its annual May Day festivities. Kinsey Jones was the head of the first PTA at the all-black school. The demographics of the county have changed dramatically over the years, and today the elementary school is predominantly white. (Timothy Jones.)

Born in Calvert County in 1916, Dan Brown was raised for several years in Washington, D.C. One day while walking across the street to milk the cows, Brown, then at the age of 12, was approached by a white lady driving a Plymouth. "Dan, I want you to come live with me," she said. Brown's father was deceased, and his mother was employed in Baltimore as a domestic worker at the time. Brown remembered, "This lady and I got in her car. . . . she told me she said she went to Baltimore, and she seen my mother ,and my mother said that she could take me. Well I never; I never had it so good in all my life. I lived in the richest section of Washington City. The very, very richest section of Washington City. It was very nice. I had my own bathroom and everything." Brown returned to Calvert in his teen years and eventually married Octavia Gross in 1937 at the home of Alfred and Etheline Gross in St. Leonard. Brown resides in Owings. (William Poe.)

116

Shortly before her passing in 2007, Virginia Hayes recalled the days of growing up on her father, Jesse Reid's, farm: "He bought this farm in 1930. My father never worked out a day in his life. He worked on the farm. My mother with us 11 children . . . she raised geese, ducks, turkeys, and chicken, poultry, and hogs. We would sell eggs, chicken . . . at the beach down here. We walked six and seven miles to go down the beach to sell vegetables and things." (William Poe.)

"I started farming, I was five. I started helping my grandfather [when] I was five years old. Dropping plants," says Russell Reid, talking about his grandfather Jesse Reid, pictured in the 2006 photograph with Russell's grandmother Lydia Jones Reid. Reid sits on the front porch of the original family farmhouse his grandfather purchased in 1930. The farm consisted of 125 acres. (William Poe.)

At the home of Florence and Oliver Sherbert, the Parran children strike a family pose in 1952. Standing in the front is Joseph; from left to right are Ralph, Carthella, and Hamilton. Uncle Carl Parran plays the piano. Joseph is currently employed with the Maryland State Comptroller's Office. Ralph retired from the Calvert County Detention Center. Carthella "Carolyn" retired from the Maryland Cooperative Extension, 4-H Club. Hamilton retired from the Food and Drug Administration (FDA) in Washington, D.C. (Gray family.)

Helen (née Morsell) and Pinkney Sewell share some time together in the kitchen of their home in Prince Frederick in the 1950s. Helen studied nursing in Baltimore. She returned to Calvert County and was a local midwife in her community. Although the Sewells owned land in the Plum Point area during the Depression era, Pinkney went to Leitch's Wharf and sharecropped for a local landowner. (Sewell family.)

This early-1960s photograph was taken at Central Elementary School in Dares Beach. The Emmanuel Seventh-day Adventist Church had given a Bible course graduation ceremony on this Saturday at the school. The church was located on Dares Beach Road across from the school. In 1959, the First Baptist Church of Prince Frederick on Dares Beach Road under J. P. Layne's leadership agreed to lease the tiny building to the Seventh-day Adventist Church. (Marsha Plater.)

Benjamin Kent Sr. is seated next to his wife, Rachel (née Morsell), in the 1920s. They were wed in 1870. Kent's father, James P. King, purchased a slave named Susanna. He fathered Benjamin, Caroline, and Thomas with Susanna. Kent lived in the house with his father while his mother, brother, and sister lived in another house up the road. Benjamin became the first Kent to purchase land—80 acres at a county tax sale. (Carrie Bertha Jones.)

This 1940s photograph was taken on the farm of Molly Jones in Plum Point. The tobacco on the back of the oxen was being hauled to a barn on the property. From left to right are (first row) Major Gross Sr., George Greene, and Leroy Greene Jr.; (second row) unidentified, Elijah Greene, (steers Tom and Donald), Leroy Greene Sr., Almous Greene, unidentified, and Norman Andrea Sr. (Darlene Harrod.)

Standing in front of the family farmhouse that his father, Allnutt Reid, purchased in 1940, Jesse Reid reflects on his dad's decision to become a school bus contractor: "Well the reason behind it, because in his area they didn't have a school bus to pick up black kids, so you know he was interested in education, so he started taking his son to school. I think he carried him a couple of years without any pay at all." (William Poe.)

Mabel (Plater) Wills of Sunderland and her husband, Guy, gave birth to Maury Wills (pictured) in 1932. Wills attended Cardoza High School in Washington, D.C., where he honed his future baseball talent. After a decade of playing in the minors, Wills finally got the chance to showcase his talents in the major league. A Los Angeles Dodger for 14 years, he led the league in stolen bases for six consecutive years. He was Major League Baseball's MVP in 1962. (Marsha Plater.)

121

For many years, Calvert County and other parts of southern Maryland relied on the tobacco crop for a large majority of the economy. In the 1990s, the Maryland government offered an incentive program to farmers that would compensate them if they stopped growing tobacco. Because of the low prices the crop was bringing at the tobacco market and the shortage of labor, many farmers accepted the buyout. These laborers at the Brady farm are cutting and spearing tobacco in 2004. (William Poe.)

Mary and Alexander Plater pose outside of their home in Sunderland in the 1930s with 10 of their 13 children and two grandchildren. Mary is believed to be of Irish descent. The Platers have traced their ancestry to Maryland governor George Plater of Sotterly Mansion in St. Mary's County. The Platers were possibly the descendants of slaves from the plantation. (Marsha Plater.)

Born in 1916, Alnutt Chase of Huntingtown reminisces about his youth: "I used to drive a truck for him [Gorman Lyons] and haul fertilizer and things down here to the farm, and I use to make three trips from Baltimore down here a day. Then, when the fertilizer season [was] over ,then he had a pick-up truck, and I used to go to people homes and carry their groceries like meal and corn and thing like that." Chase, a devoted church man, imparts his wisdom: "Well, it's just the way you live. The way you live is the way you gonna die. If you live and treat people right, you gonna die right. And if you live wrong, then you can die wrong. . . . because I know one thing, that day is coming. One day, sooner or later, we got to leave here and gonna leave here, and you better be ready when you leave." (Both, William Poe.)

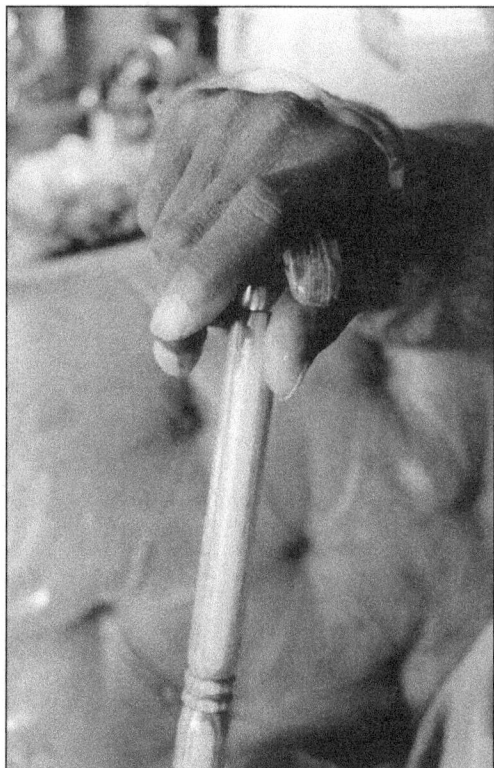

Outside their home in Sunderland, Myrtle and Warren Plater strike a 1950s pose. Their property on Claggett Road was originally a tobacco farm and has since been subdivided for housing for their grandchildren. Plater was a stay-at-home mother who, later in life, took a job as a cook in the beach area. Warren was a farmer and a building contractor. (Marsha Plater.)

Elmer Columbus Ray is pictured in the 1950s in one of his farm trucks he used when hauling tobacco to the market. Ray, a tobacco farmer, also worked for local farmer and businessman Clyde Jones. Ray would transport truckloads of goods to Baltimore for Jones. (Eloise Ray.)

Pictured in 2006, Lemuel (at right) and Lillian (Ford) Adams (below, third from left) met in 1945. The couple shared this story from the front porch of where Ford grew up and where the couple continues to reside: "We met at his mother's house cause I was friends with his sister. I was 18. You didn't go out until you were 18 unless you stole out. We went to the movies. The colored people were upstairs and the white downstairs." Lemuel recalls, "When I met Mrs. Adams that looked like that was the day. That was it. I just went to talk to Mr. Ford to see what he had to say. Then it was up to me." The couple will celebrate their 63rd wedding anniversary in 2008. Pictured from left to right below are daughter Bertina, daughter Anna, Lillian Adams, granddaughter Priscilla, and daughter Adelia on Mother's Day in 2007. (William Poe.)

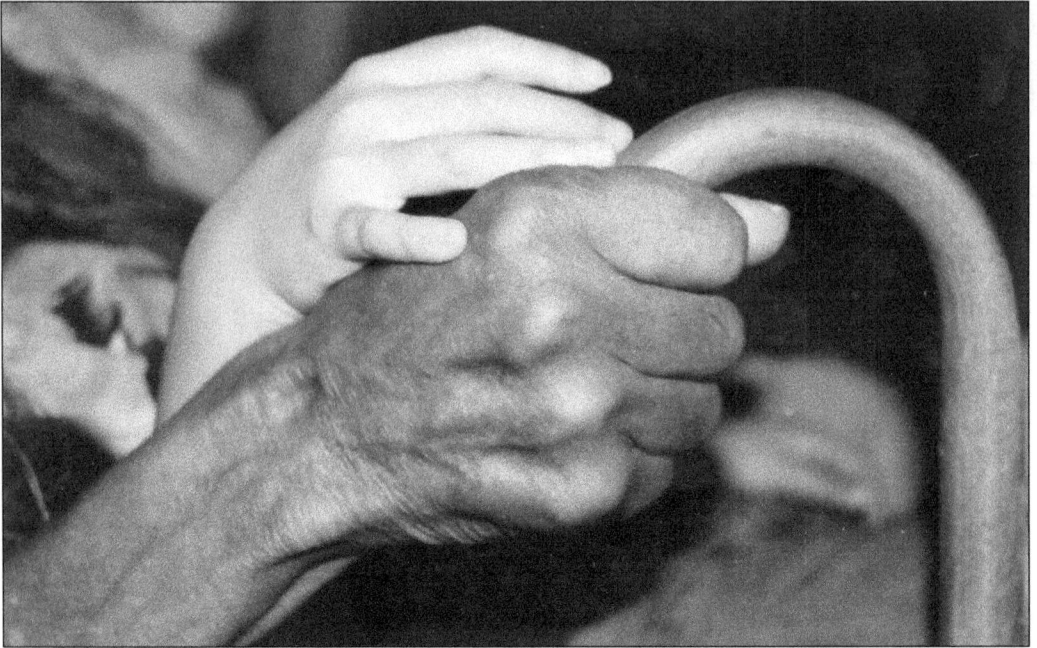

Enoch Tyler was a storyteller by nature. In the photograph above, he sits with the author's daughter, Audrey, age 9 at the time, and shares some of his life's wisdom: "Treat everybody like you would like to be treated. And them that couldn't stand it, don't pay him no mind, don't fool around with him, don't let him lead you in no trouble, but whatever is right you try to do it." The attendance at his funeral was similar to what would be expected of a dignitary's passing. All ages of people came to pay their final respects to a pillar of the community. There were no mourners on this day, only a gathering of celebrators paying homage to a well-respected elder. Tyler was laid to rest at Young's Methodist Church. (Both, William Poe.)

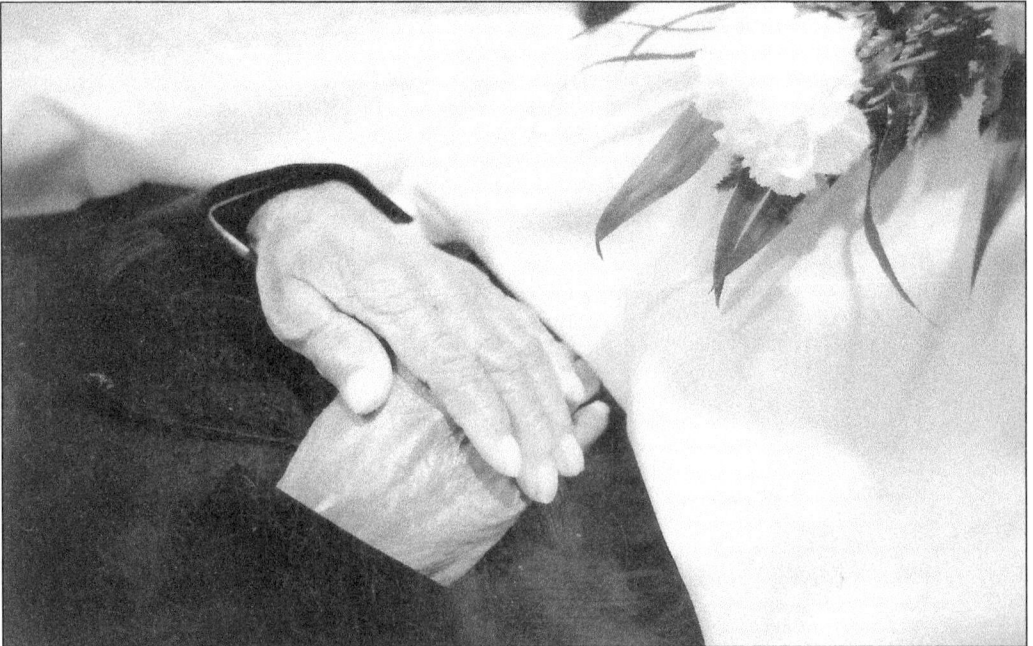

Battling cancer at the time of this 2006 photograph, Oliver Foote (right) closed his interview on this day with a passage from his childhood: "I thinks when I read this story of old, when Jesus was here among mens, how he called little childrens as lambs to his fold, I would like to have been with him then, I wished that his hands had been placed on my head, and his arms they were thrown around me, and if I though heard his great word when he said, let the little one's come unto me. And yet to his foot stool and prayers I may go, and ask for a share of his love, and if I though earnestly seek him below, I shall see him and hear him above." William Poe is pictured with Foote. (William Poe.)

ACROSS AMERICA, PEOPLE ARE DISCOVERING SOMETHING WONDERFUL. *THEIR HERITAGE.*

Arcadia Publishing is the leading local history publisher in the United States. With more than 4,000 titles in print and hundreds of new titles released every year, Arcadia has extensive specialized experience chronicling the history of communities and celebrating America's hidden stories, bringing to life the people, places, and events from the past. To discover the history of other communities across the nation, please visit:

www.arcadiapublishing.com

Customized search tools allow you to find regional history books about the town where you grew up, the cities where your friends and family live, the town where your parents met, or even that retirement spot you've been dreaming about.

www.ingramcontent.com/pod-product-compliance
Lightning Source LLC
Chambersburg PA
CBHW061750260326
41914CB00006B/1058